HOLT SCIENCE & TECHNOLOGY

Introduction to Matter

HOLT, RINEHART AND WINSTON

A Harcourt Education Company

Orlando • **Austin** • New York • San Diego • Toronto • London

Acknowledgments

Contributing Authors

Mapi Cuevas, Ph.D.
Professor of Chemistry
Department of Natural Sciences
Santa Fe Community College
Gainesville, Florida

Sally Ann Vonderbrink, Ph.D.
Chemistry Teacher
(retired)
Cincinnati, Ohio

Inclusion and Special Needs Consultant

Ellen McPeek Glisan
Special Needs Consultant
San Antonio, Texas

Safety Reviewer

Jack Gerlovich, Ph.D.
Associate Professor
School of Education
Drake University
Des Moines, Iowa

Academic Reviewers

Scott Darveau, Ph.D.
Assistant Professor of Chemistry
Chemistry Department
University of Nebraska at Kearney
Kearney, Nebraska

Cassandra Eagle, Ph.D.
Professor of Organic Chemistry
Chemistry Department
Appalachian State University
Boone, North Carolina

Mark N. Kobrak, Ph.D.
Assistant Professor of Chemistry
Chemistry Department
Brooklyn College of the City University of New York
Brooklyn, New York

Daniela Kohen, Ph.D.
Assistant Professor of Chemistry
Chemistry Department
Carleton College
Northfield, Minnesota

Enrique Peacock-López, Ph.D.
Professor of Chemistry
Department of Chemistry
Williams College
Williamstown, Massachusetts

Kate Queeney, Ph.D.
Assistant Professor of Chemistry
Chemistry Department
Smith College
Northampton, Massachusetts

Richard S. Treptow, Ph.D.
Professor of Chemistry
Department of Chemistry and Physics
Chicago State University
Chicago, Illinois

Dale Wheeler
Associate Professor of Chemistry
A. R. Smith Department of Chemistry
Appalachian State University
Boone, North Carolina

Lab Testing

Paul Boyle
Science Teacher
Perry Heights Middle School
Evansville, Indiana

C. John Graves
Science Teacher
Monforton Middle School
Bozeman, Montana

Norman E. Holcomb
Science Teacher
Marion Elementary School
Marion, Ohio

Kenneth J. Horn
Science Teacher and Dept. Chair
Fallston Middle School
Fallston, Maryland

Alyson M. Mike
Science Teacher and Department Chair
East Valley Middle School
East Helena, Montana

Joseph W. Price
Science Teacher and Department Chair
H.M. Browne Junior High School
Washington, D.C.

Sharon L. Woolf
Science Teacher
Langston Hughes Middle School
Reston, Virginia

Lee Yassinski
Science Teacher
Sun Valley Middle School
Sun Valley, California

Printed in the United States of America

ISBN 0-03-050092-3

4 5 6 7 048 09 08 07

K Introduction to Matter

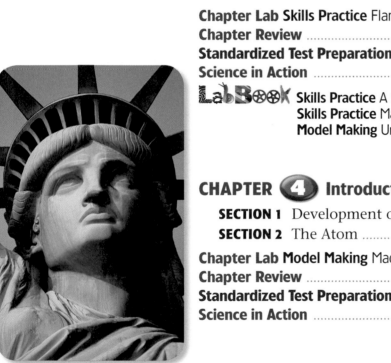

Labs and Activities

PRE-READING ACTIVITY

START-UP ACTIVITY

Quick Lab

Labs

INTERNET ACTIVITY

Go to go.hrw.com and type in the red keyword.

SCHOOL to HOME

READING STRATEGY

How to Use Your Textbook

Your Roadmap for Success with Holt Science and Technology

What You Will Learn

At the beginning of every section you will find the section's objectives and vocabulary terms. The objectives tell you what you'll need to know after you finish reading the section.

Vocabulary terms are listed for each section. Learn the definitions of these terms because you will most likely be tested on them. Each term is highlighted in the text and is defined at point of use and in the margin. You can also use the glossary to locate definitions quickly.

STUDY TIP Reread the objectives and the definitions to the terms when studying for a test to be sure you know the material.

Get Organized

A Reading Strategy at the beginning of every section provides tips to help you organize and remember the information covered in the section. Keep a science notebook so that you are ready to take notes when your teacher reviews the material in class. Keep your assignments in this notebook so that you can review them when studying for the chapter test.

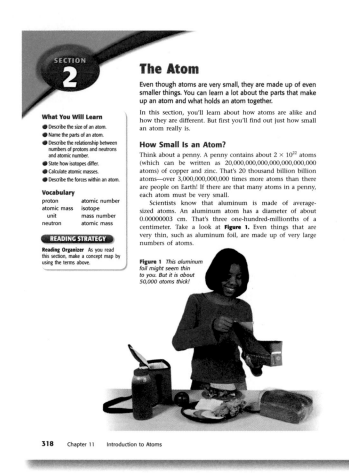

SECTION 2

The Atom

Even though atoms are very small, they are made up of even smaller things. You can learn a lot about the parts that make up an atom and what holds an atom together.

In this section, you'll learn about how atoms are alike and how they are different. But first you'll find out just how small an atom really is.

How Small Is an Atom?

Think about a penny. A penny contains about 2×10^{22} atoms (which can be written as 20,000,000,000,000,000,000,000 atoms) of copper and zinc. That's 20 thousand billion billion atoms—over 3,000,000,000,000 times more atoms than there are people on Earth! If there are that many atoms in a penny, each atom must be very small.

Scientists know that aluminum is made of average-sized atoms. An aluminum atom has a diameter of about 0.00000003 cm. That's three one-hundred-millionths of a centimeter. Take a look at **Figure 1**. Even things that are very thin, such as aluminum foil, are made up of very large numbers of atoms.

Figure 1 This aluminum foil might seem thin to you. But it is about 50,000 atoms thick!

What You Will Learn

- Describe the size of an atom.
- Name the parts of an atom.
- Describe the relationship between numbers of protons and neutrons and atomic number.
- State how isotopes differ.
- Calculate atomic masses.
- Describe the forces within an atom.

Vocabulary

proton   atomic number
atomic mass   isotope
   unit   mass number
neutron   atomic mass

READING STRATEGY

Reading Organizer As you read this section, make a concept map by using the terms above.

318   Chapter 11   Introduction to Atoms

⬈ Be Resourceful—Use the Web

SciLinks boxes in your textbook take you to resources that you can use for science projects, reports, and research papers. Go to **scilinks.org** and type in the **SciLinks code** to find information on a topic.

Visit go.hrw.com
Check out the **Current Science®** magazine articles and other materials that go with your textbook at **go.hrw.com.** Click on the textbook icon and the table of contents to see all of the resources for each chapter.

Use the Illustrations and Photos

Art shows complex ideas and processes. Learn to analyze the art so that you better understand the material you read in the text.

Tables and graphs display important information in an organized way to help you see relationships.

A picture is worth a thousand words. Look at the photographs to see relevant examples of science concepts that you are reading about.

Answer the Section Reviews

Section Reviews test your knowledge of the main points of the section. Critical Thinking items challenge you to think about the material in greater depth and to find connections that you infer from the text.

STUDY TIP When you can't answer a question, reread the section. The answer is usually there.

Do Your Homework

Your teacher may assign worksheets to help you understand and remember the material in the chapter.

STUDY TIP Don't try to answer the questions without reading the text and reviewing your class notes. A little preparation up front will make your homework assignments a lot easier. Answering the items in the Chapter Review will help prepare you for the chapter test.

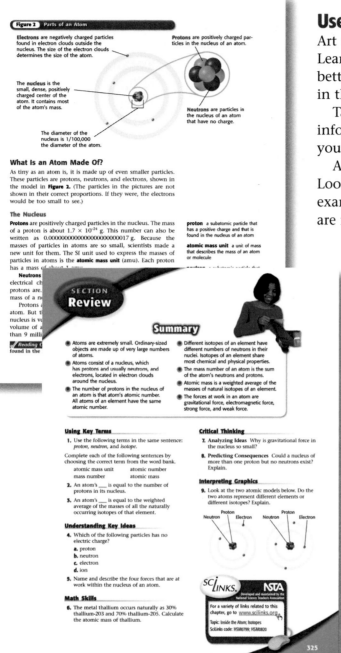

Visit Holt Online Learning

If your teacher gives you a special password to log onto the **Holt Online Learning** site, you'll find your complete textbook on the Web. In addition, you'll find some great learning tools and practice quizzes. You'll be able to see how well you know the material from your textbook.

SAFETY FIRST!

Exploring, inventing, and investigating are essential to the study of science. However, these activities can also be dangerous. To make sure that your experiments and explorations are safe, you must be aware of a variety of safety guidelines. You have probably heard of the saying, "It is better to be safe than sorry." This is particularly true in a science classroom where experiments and explorations are being performed. Being uninformed and careless can result in serious injuries. Don't take chances with your own safety or with anyone else's.

The following pages describe important guidelines for staying safe in the science classroom. Your teacher may also have safety guidelines and tips that are specific to your classroom and laboratory. Take the time to be safe.

Safety Rules!

Start Out Right

Always get your teacher's permission before attempting any laboratory exploration. Read the procedures carefully, and pay particular attention to safety information and caution statements. If you are unsure about what a safety symbol means, look it up or ask your teacher. You cannot be too careful when it comes to safety. If an accident does occur, inform your teacher immediately regardless of how minor you think the accident is.

If you are instructed to note the odor of a substance, wave the fumes toward your nose with your hand. Never put your nose close to the source.

Safety Symbols

All of the experiments and investigations in this book and their related worksheets include important safety symbols to alert you to particular safety concerns. Become familiar with these symbols so that when you see them, you will know what they mean and what to do. It is important that you read this entire safety section to learn about specific dangers in the laboratory.

Eye protection

Clothing protection

Hand safety

Heating safety

Electric safety

Chemical safety

Animal safety

Sharp object

Plant safety

x

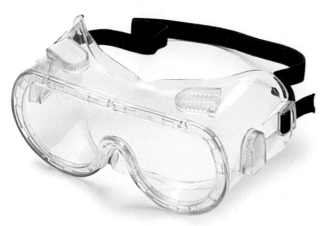

Eye Safety

Wear safety goggles when working around chemicals, acids, bases, or any type of flame or heating device. Wear safety goggles any time there is even the slightest chance that harm could come to your eyes. If any substance gets into your eyes, notify your teacher immediately and flush your eyes with running water for at least 15 minutes. Treat any unknown chemical as if it were a dangerous chemical. Never look directly into the sun. Doing so could cause permanent blindness.

Avoid wearing contact lenses in a laboratory situation. Even if you are wearing safety goggles, chemicals can get between the contact lenses and your eyes. If your doctor requires that you wear contact lenses instead of glasses, wear eye-cup safety goggles in the lab.

Safety Equipment

Know the locations of the nearest fire alarms and any other safety equipment, such as fire blankets and eyewash fountains, as identified by your teacher, and know the procedures for using the equipment.

Neatness

Keep your work area free of all unnecessary books and papers. Tie back long hair, and secure loose sleeves or other loose articles of clothing, such as ties and bows. Remove dangling jewelry. Don't wear open-toed shoes or sandals in the laboratory. Never eat, drink, or apply cosmetics in a laboratory setting. Food, drink, and cosmetics can easily become contaminated with dangerous materials.

Certain hair products (such as aerosol hair spray) are flammable and should not be worn while working near an open flame. Avoid wearing hair spray or hair gel on lab days.

Sharp/Pointed Objects

Use knives and other sharp instruments with extreme care. Never cut objects while holding them in your hands. Place objects on a suitable work surface for cutting.

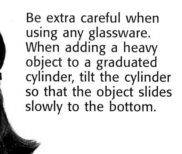

Be extra careful when using any glassware. When adding a heavy object to a graduated cylinder, tilt the cylinder so that the object slides slowly to the bottom.

Chemicals

Wear safety goggles when handling any potentially dangerous chemicals, acids, or bases. If a chemical is unknown, handle it as you would a dangerous chemical. Wear an apron and protective gloves when you work with acids or bases or whenever you are told to do so. If a spill gets on your skin or clothing, rinse it off immediately with water for at least 5 minutes while calling to your teacher.

Never mix chemicals unless your teacher tells you to do so. Never taste, touch, or smell chemicals unless you are specifically directed to do so. Before working with a flammable liquid or gas, check for the presence of any source of flame, spark, or heat.

Heat

Wear safety goggles when using a heating device or a flame. Whenever possible, use an electric hot plate as a heat source instead of using an open flame. When heating materials in a test tube, always angle the test tube away from yourself and others. To avoid burns, wear heat-resistant gloves whenever instructed to do so.

Electricity

Be careful with electrical cords. When using a microscope with a lamp, do not place the cord where it could trip someone. Do not let cords hang over a table edge in a way that could cause equipment to fall if the cord is accidentally pulled. Do not use equipment with damaged cords. Be sure that your hands are dry and that the electrical equipment is in the "off" position before plugging it in. Turn off and unplug electrical equipment when you are finished.

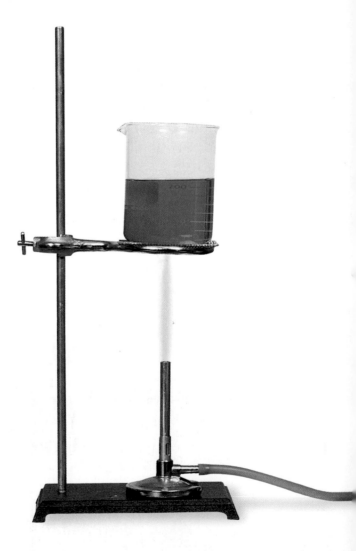

Animal Safety

Always obtain your teacher's permission before bringing any animal into the school building. Handle animals only as your teacher directs. Always treat animals carefully and respectfully. Wash your hands thoroughly after handling any animal.

Plant Safety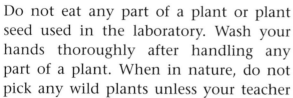

Do not eat any part of a plant or plant seed used in the laboratory. Wash your hands thoroughly after handling any part of a plant. When in nature, do not pick any wild plants unless your teacher instructs you to do so.

Glassware

Examine all glassware before use. Be sure that glassware is clean and free of chips and cracks. Report damaged glassware to your teacher. Glass containers used for heating should be made of heat-resistant glass.

1

The Properties of Matter

The Big Idea

Matter is described by its properties and may undergo changes.

About the PHOTO

This giant ice dragon began as a 1,700 kg block of ice! Making the blocks of ice takes six weeks. Then, the ice blocks are stored at −30°C until the sculpting begins. The artist has to work at −10°C to keep the ice from melting. An ice sculptor has to be familiar with the many properties of water, including its melting point.

PRE-READING ACTIVITY

FOLDNOTES **Booklet** Before you read the chapter, create the FoldNote entitled "Booklet" described in the **Study Skills** section of the Appendix. Label each page of the booklet with a main idea from the chapter. As you read the chapter, write what you learn about each main idea on the appropriate page of the booklet.

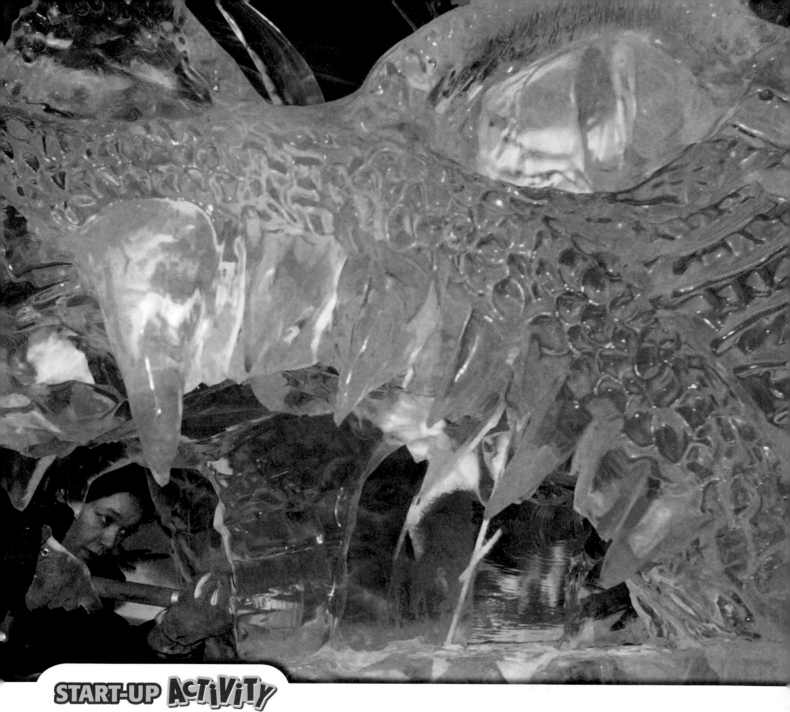

START-UP ACTiViTY

Sack Secrets

In this activity, you will test your skills in determining an object's identity based on the object's properties.

Procedure

1. You and two or three of your classmates will receive a **sealed paper sack** containing a **mystery object.** Do not open the sack!

2. For five minutes, make as many observations about the object as you can without opening the sack. You may touch, smell, shake, or listen to the object through the sack. Record your observations.

Analysis

1. At the end of five minutes, discuss your findings with your partners.

2. List the object's properties that you can identify. Make another list of properties that you cannot identify. Make a conclusion about the object's identity.

3. Share your observations, your list of properties, and your conclusion with the class. Then, open the sack.

4. Did you properly identify the object? If so, how? If not, why not? Record your answers.

What Is Matter?

What do you have in common with a toaster, a steaming bowl of soup, or a bright neon sign?

You are probably thinking that this is a trick question. It is hard to imagine that a person has anything in common with a kitchen appliance, hot soup, or a glowing neon sign.

Matter

From a scientific point of view, you have at least one characteristic in common with these things. You, the toaster, the bowl, the soup, the steam, the glass tubing of a neon sign, and the glowing gas are made of matter. But exactly what is matter? **Matter** is anything that has mass and takes up space. It's that simple! Everything in the universe that you can see is made up of some type of matter.

Matter and Volume

All matter takes up space. The amount of space taken up, or occupied, by an object is known as the object's **volume.** Your fingernails, the Statue of Liberty, the continent of Africa, and a cloud have volume. And because these things have volume, they cannot share the same space at the same time. Even the tiniest speck of dust takes up space. Another speck of dust cannot fit into that space without somehow bumping the first speck out of the way. **Figure 1** shows an example of how one object cannot share with another object the same space at the same time. Try the Quick Lab on the next page to see for yourself that matter takes up space.

What You Will Learn

● Describe the two properties of all matter.
● Identify the units used to measure volume and mass.
● Compare mass and weight.
● Explain the relationship between mass and inertia.

Vocabulary

matter	mass
volume	weight
meniscus	inertia

READING STRATEGY

Prediction Guide Before reading this section, write the title of each heading in this section. Next, under each heading, write what you think you will learn.

matter anything that has mass and takes up space

volume a measure of the size of a body or region in three-dimensional space

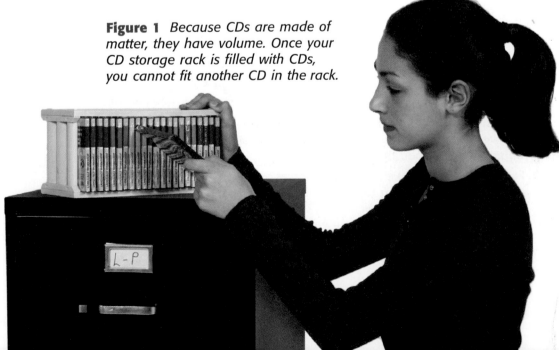

Figure 1 *Because CDs are made of matter, they have volume. Once your CD storage rack is filled with CDs, you cannot fit another CD in the rack.*

Quick Lab

Space Case

1. Crumple a **piece of paper.** Fit it tightly in the bottom of a **clear plastic cup** so that it won't fall out.
2. Turn the cup upside down. Lower the cup straight down into a **bucket** half-filled with **water.** Be sure that the cup is completely underwater.
3. Lift the cup straight out of the water. Turn the cup upright, and observe the paper. Record your observations.
4. Use the point of a **pencil** to punch a small hole in the bottom of the cup. Repeat steps 2 and 3.
5. How do the results show that air has volume? Explain your answer.

Liquid Volume

Lake Erie, the smallest of the Great Lakes, has a volume of approximately 483 trillion (that's 483,000,000,000,000) liters of water. Can you imagine that much water? Think of a 2-liter bottle of soda. The water in Lake Erie could fill more than 241 trillion 2-liter soda bottles. That's a lot of water! On a smaller scale, a can of soda has a volume of only 355 milliliters, which is about one-third of a liter. You can check the volume of the soda by using a large measuring cup from your kitchen.

Liters (L) and milliliters (mL) are the units used most often to express the volume of liquids. The volume of any amount of liquid, from one raindrop to a can of soda to an entire ocean, can be expressed in these units.

✓ Reading Check What are two units used to measure volume? (*See the Appendix for answers to Reading Checks.*)

Measuring the Volume of Liquids

In your science class, you'll probably use a graduated cylinder instead of a measuring cup to measure the volume of liquids. Graduated cylinders are used to measure the liquid volume when accuracy is important. The surface of a liquid in any container, including a measuring cup or a large beaker, is curved. The curve at the surface of a liquid is called a **meniscus** (muh NIS kuhs). To measure the volume of most liquids, such as water, you must look at the bottom of the meniscus, as shown in **Figure 2.** Note that you may not be able to see a meniscus in a large beaker. The meniscus looks flat because the liquid is in a wide container.

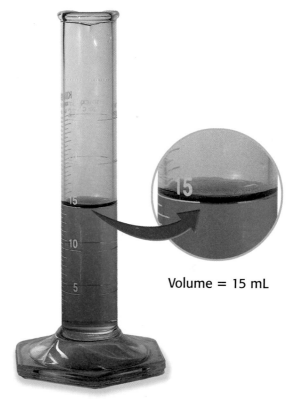

Volume = 15 mL

Figure 2 *To measure volume correctly, read the scale of the lowest part of the meniscus (as shown) at eye level.*

meniscus the curve at a liquid's surface by which one measures the volume of the liquid

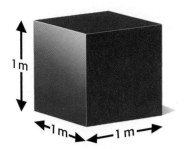

Figure 3 *A cubic meter (1 m³) is a cube that has a length, width, and height of 1 m.*

Volume of a Regularly Shaped Solid Object

The volume of any solid object is expressed in cubic units. The word *cubic* means "having three dimensions." In science, cubic meters (m^3) and cubic centimeters (cm^3) are the units most often used to express the volume of solid things. The 3 in these unit symbols shows that three quantities, or dimensions, were multiplied to get the final result. You can see the three dimensions of a cubic meter in **Figure 3.** There are formulas to find the volume of regularly shaped objects. For example, to find the volume of a cube or a rectangular object, multiply the length, width, and height of the object, as shown in the following equation:

$$volume = length \times width \times height$$

Volume of an Irregularly Shaped Solid Object

How do you find the volume of a solid that does not have a regular shape? For example, to find the volume of a 12-sided object, you cannot use the equation given above. But you can measure the volume of a solid object by measuring the volume of water that the object displaces. In **Figure 4,** when a 12-sided object is added to the water in a graduated cylinder, the water level rises. The volume of water displaced by the object is equal to its volume. Because 1 mL is equal to 1 cm^3, you can express the volume of the water displaced by the object in cubic centimeters. Although volumes of liquids can be expressed in cubic units, volumes of solids should not be expressed in liters or milliliters.

Figure 4 *The 12-sided object displaced 15 mL of water. Because 1 mL = 1 cm³, the volume of the object is 15 cm³.*

✓ Reading Check Explain how you would measure the volume of an apple.

MATH FOCUS

Volume of a Rectangular Solid What is the volume of a box that has a length of 5 cm, a width of 1 cm, and a height of 2 cm?

Step 1: Write the equation for volume.

$$volume = length \times width \times height$$

Step 2: Replace the variables with the measurements given to you, and solve.

$$volume = 5 \text{ cm} \times 1 \text{ cm} \times 2 \text{ cm} = 10 \text{ cm}^3$$

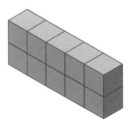

Now It's Your Turn
1. A book has a length of 25 cm, a width of 18 cm, and a height of 4 cm. What is its volume?
2. What is the volume of a suitcase that has a length of 95 cm, a width of 50 cm, and a height of 20 cm?
3. A CD case is 14.2 cm long, 12.4 cm wide, and 1 cm deep. What is its volume?

Matter and Mass

Another characteristic of all matter is mass. **Mass** is the amount of matter in an object. For example, you and a peanut are made of matter. But you are made of more matter than a peanut is, so you have more mass. The mass of an object is the same no matter where in the universe the object is located. The only way to change the mass of an object is to change the amount of matter that makes up the object.

mass a measure of the amount of matter in an object

weight a measure of the gravitational force exerted on an object; its value can change with the location of the object in the universe

The Difference Between Mass and Weight

The terms *mass* and *weight* are often used as though they mean the same thing, but they don't. **Weight** is a measure of the gravitational (GRAV i TAY shuh nuhl) force exerted on an object. Gravitational force keeps objects on Earth from floating into space. The gravitational force between an object and the Earth depends partly on the object's mass. The more mass an object has, the greater the gravitational force on the object and the greater the object's weight. But an object's weight can change depending on its location in the universe. An object would weigh less on the moon than it does on Earth because the moon has less gravitational force than Earth does. **Figure 5** explains the differences between mass and weight.

Figure 5 Differences Between Mass and Weight

Mass	Weight
• Mass is a measure of the amount of matter in an object.	• Weight is a measure of the gravitational force on an object.
• Mass is always constant for an object no matter where the object is located in the universe.	• Weight varies depending on where the object is in relation to the Earth (or any large body in the universe).
• Mass is measured by using a balance (shown below).	• Weight is measured by using a spring scale (shown at right).
• Mass is expressed in kilograms (kg), grams (g), and milligrams (mg).	• Weight is expressed in newtons (N).

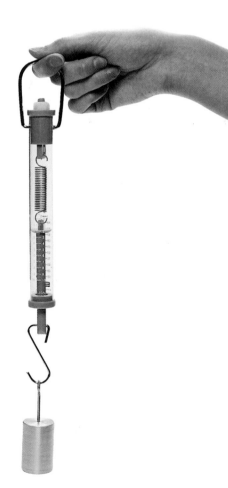

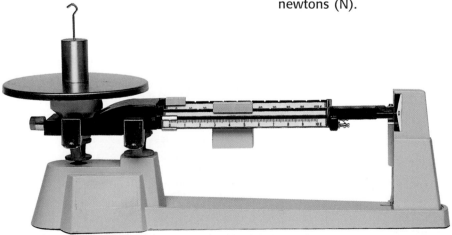

Figure 6 *The brick and the sponge take up the same amount of space. But the brick has more matter in it, so its mass—and thus its weight—is greater.*

inertia the tendency of an object to resist being moved or, if the object is moving, to resist a change in speed or direction until an outside force acts on the object

Measuring Mass and Weight

The brick and the sponge in **Figure 6** have the same volume. But because the brick has more mass, a greater gravitational force is exerted on the brick than on the sponge. As a result, the brick weighs more than the sponge.

The SI unit of mass is the kilogram (kg), but mass is often expressed in grams (g) and milligrams (mg), too. These units can be used to express the mass of any object in the universe.

Weight is a measure of gravitational force and is expressed in the SI unit of force, the *newton* (N). One newton is about equal to the weight of an object that has a mass of 100 g on Earth. So, if you know the mass of an object, you can calculate the object's weight on Earth. Weight is a good estimate of the mass of an object because, on Earth, gravity doesn't change.

✓ *Reading Check* **What units are often used to measure mass?**

Inertia

Imagine kicking a soccer ball that has the mass of a bowling ball. It would be not only painful but also very difficult to get the ball moving in the first place! The reason is inertia (in UHR shuh). **Inertia** is the tendency of an object to resist a change in motion. So, an object at rest will remain at rest until something causes the object to move. Also, a moving object will keep moving at the same speed and in the same direction unless something acts on the object to change its speed or direction.

Converting Mass to Weight A student has a mass of 45,000 g. How much does this student weigh in newtons?

Step 1: Write the information given to you.

$$45,000 \text{ g}$$

Step 2: Write the conversion factor to change grams into newtons.

$$1 \text{ N} = 100 \text{ g}$$

Step 3: Write the equation so that grams will cancel.

$$45,000 \text{ g} \times \frac{1 \text{ N}}{100 \text{ g}} = 450 \text{ N}$$

Now It's Your Turn

1. What is the weight of a car that has a mass of 1,362,000 g?
2. Your pair of boots has a mass of 850 g. If each boot has exactly the same mass, what is the weight of each boot?

Mass: The Measure of Inertia

Mass is a measure of inertia. An object that has a large mass is harder to get moving and harder to stop than an object that has less mass. The reason is that the object with the large mass has greater inertia. For example, imagine that you are going to push a grocery cart that has only one potato in it. Pushing the cart is easy because the mass and inertia are small. But suppose the grocery cart is stacked with potatoes, as in **Figure 7.** Now the total mass—and the inertia—of the cart full of potatoes is much greater. It will be harder to get the cart moving. And once the cart is moving, stopping the cart will be harder.

Figure 7 *Because of inertia, moving a cart full of potatoes is more difficult than moving a cart that is empty.*

SECTION Review

Summary

- Two properties of matter are volume and mass.
- Volume is the amount of space taken up by an object.
- The SI unit of volume is the liter (L).
- Mass is the amount of matter in an object.
- The SI unit of mass is the kilogram (kg).
- Weight is a measure of the gravitational force on an object, usually in relation to the Earth.
- Inertia is the tendency of an object to resist being moved or, if the object is moving, to resist a change in speed or direction. The more massive an object is, the greater its inertia.

Using Key Terms

1. Use the following terms in the same sentence: *volume* and *meniscus.*

2. In your own words, write a definition for each of the following terms: *mass, weight,* and *inertia.*

Understanding Key Ideas

3. Which of the following is matter?
   - **a.** dust
   - **b.** the moon
   - **c.** strand of hair
   - **d.** All of the above

4. A graduated cylinder is used to measure
   - **a.** volume.
   - **b.** weight.
   - **c.** mass.
   - **d.** inertia.

5. The volume of a solid is measured in
   - **a.** liters.
   - **b.** grams.
   - **c.** cubic centimeters.
   - **d.** All of the above

6. Mass is measured in
   - **a.** liters.
   - **b.** centimeters.
   - **c.** newtons.
   - **d.** kilograms.

7. Explain the relationship between mass and inertia.

Math Skills

8. A nugget of gold is placed in a graduated cylinder that contains 80 mL of water. The water level rises to 225 mL after the nugget is added to the cylinder. What is the volume of the gold nugget?

9. One newton equals about 100 g on Earth. How many newtons would a football weigh if it had a mass of 400 g?

Critical Thinking

10. **Identifying Relationships** Do objects with large masses always have large weights? Explain.

11. **Applying Concepts** Would an elephant weigh more or less on the moon than it would weigh on Earth? Explain your answer.

SCILINKS ®

NSTA

Developed and maintained by the National Science Teachers Association

For a variety of links related to this chapter, go to www.scilinks.org

Topic: What Is Matter?
SciLinks code: HSM1662

Physical Properties

Have you ever played the game 20 Questions? The goal of this game is to figure out what object another person is thinking of by asking 20 yes/no questions or less.

If you can't figure out the object's identity after asking 20 questions, you may not be asking the right kinds of questions. What kinds of questions should you ask? You may want to ask questions about the physical properties of the object. Knowing the properties of an object can help you find out what it is.

Physical Properties

The questions in **Figure 1** help someone gather information about color, odor, mass, and volume. Each piece of information is a physical property of matter. A **physical property** of matter can be observed or measured without changing the matter's identity. For example, you don't have to change an apple's identity to see its color or to measure its volume.

Other physical properties, such as magnetism, the ability to conduct electric current, strength, and flexibility, can help someone identify how to use a substance. For example, think of a scooter with an electric motor. The magnetism produced by the motor is used to convert energy stored in a battery into energy that will turn the wheels.

✓ Reading Check List four physical properties. (*See the Appendix for answers to Reading Checks.*)

What You Will Learn

- Identify six examples of physical properties of matter.
- Describe how density is used to identify substances.
- List six examples of physical changes.
- Explain what happens to matter during a physical change.

Vocabulary

physical property
density
physical change

READING STRATEGY

Mnemonics As you read this section, create a mnemonic device to help you remember examples of physical properties.

Could I hold it in my hand? **Yes.**
Does it have an odor? **Yes.**
Is it safe to eat? **Yes.**
Is it orange? **No.**
Is it yellow? **No.**
Is it red? **Yes.**
Is it an apple? **Yes!**

Figure 1 *Asking questions about the physical properties of an object can help you identify it.*

Figure 2 Examples of Physical Properties

Thermal conductivity (KAHN duhk TIV uh tee) is the rate at which a substance transfers heat. Plastic foam is a poor conductor.

State is the physical form in which a substance exists, such as a solid, liquid, or gas. Ice is water in the solid state.

Density is the mass per unit volume of a substance. Lead is very dense, so it makes a good sinker for a fishing line.

Solubility (SAHL yoo BIL uh tee) is the ability of a substance to dissolve in another substance. Flavored drink mix dissolves in water.

Ductility (duhk TIL uh tee) is the ability of a substance to be pulled into a wire. Copper is often used to make wiring because it is ductile.

Malleability (MAL ee uh BIL uh tee) is the ability of a substance to be rolled or pounded into thin sheets. Aluminum can be rolled into sheets to make foil.

Identifying Matter

You use physical properties every day. For example, physical properties help you determine if your socks are clean (odor), if your books will fit into your backpack (volume), or if your shirt matches your pants (color). **Figure 2** gives more examples of physical properties.

Density

Density is a physical property that describes the relationship between mass and volume. **Density** is the amount of matter in a given space, or volume. A golf ball and a table-tennis ball, such as those in **Figure 3**, have similar volumes. But a golf ball has more mass than a table-tennis ball does. So, the golf ball has a greater density.

physical property a characteristic of a substance that does not involve a chemical change, such as density, color, or hardness

density the ratio of the mass of a substance to the volume of the substance

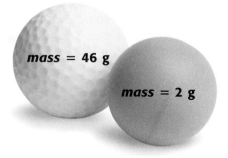

mass = 46 g

mass = 2 g

Figure 3 *A golf ball is denser than a table-tennis ball because the golf ball contains more matter in a similar volume.*

Liquid Layers

What do you think causes the liquid in **Figure 4** to look the way it does? Is it trick photography? No, it is differences in density! There are six liquids in the graduated cylinder. Each liquid has a different density. If the liquids are carefully poured into the cylinder, they can form six layers because of the differences in density. The densest layer is on the bottom. The least dense layer is on top. The order of the layers shows the order of increasing density. Yellow is the least dense, followed by the colorless layer, red, blue, green, and brown (the densest).

Density of Solids

Which would you rather carry around all day: a kilogram of lead or a kilogram of feathers? At first, you might say feathers. But both the feathers and the lead have the same mass, just as the cotton balls and the tomatoes have the same mass, as shown in **Figure 5.** So, the lead would be less awkward to carry around than the feathers would. The feathers are much less dense than the lead. So, it takes a lot of feathers to equal the same mass of lead.

Knowing the density of a substance can also tell you if the substance will float or sink in water. If the density of an object is less than the density of water, the object will float. Likewise, a solid object whose density is greater than the density of water will sink when the object is placed in water.

Reading Check What will happen to an object placed in water if the object's density is less than water's density?

Figure 4 *This graduated cylinder contains six liquids. From top to bottom, they are corn oil, water, shampoo, dish detergent, antifreeze, and maple syrup.*

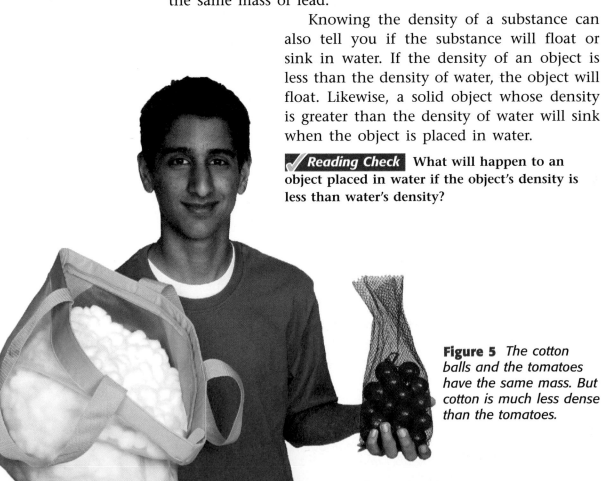

Figure 5 *The cotton balls and the tomatoes have the same mass. But cotton is much less dense than the tomatoes.*

Solving for Density

To find an object's density (D), first measure its mass (m) and volume (V). Then, use the equation below.

$$D = \frac{m}{V}$$

Units for density consist of a mass unit divided by a volume unit. Some units for density are g/cm^3, g/mL, kg/m^3, and kg/L. Remember that the volume of a solid is often given in cubic centimeters or cubic meters. So, the density of a solid should be given in units of g/cm^3 or kg/m^3.

Using Density to Identify Substances

Density is a useful physical property for identifying substances. Each substance has a density that differs from the densities of other substances. And the density of a substance is always the same at a given temperature and pressure. Look at **Table 1** to compare the densities of several common substances.

Twenty Questions

Play a game of 20 Questions with an adult. One person will think of an object, and the other person will ask yes/no questions about it. Write the questions in your **science journal** as you play. Put a check mark next to the questions asked about physical properties. When the object is identified or when the 20 questions are up, switch roles.

Table 1 Densities of Common Substances*			
Substance	**Density* (g/cm^3)**	**Substance**	**Density* (g/cm^3)**
Helium (gas)	0.0001663	Zinc (solid)	7.13
Oxygen (gas)	0.001331	Silver (solid)	10.50
Water (liquid)	1.00	Lead (solid)	11.35
Pyrite (solid)	5.02	Mercury (liquid)	13.55

*at 20°C and 1.0 atm

Calculating Density What is the density of an object whose mass is 25 g and whose volume is 10 cm^3?

Step 1: Write the equation for density.

$$D = \frac{m}{V}$$

Step 2: Replace m and V with the measurements given in the problem, and solve.

$$D = \frac{25 \text{ g}}{10 \text{ cm}^3} = 2.5 \text{ g/cm}^3$$

The equation for density can also be rearranged to find mass and volume, as shown.

$m = D \times V$ (Rearrange by multiplying by V.)

$V = \frac{m}{D}$ (Rearrange by dividing by D.)

Now It's Your Turn

1. Find the density of a substance that has a mass of 45 kg and a volume of 43 m^3. (Hint: Make sure your answer's units are units of density.)
2. Suppose you have a lead ball whose mass is 454 g. What is the ball's volume? (Hint: Use **Table 1** above.)
3. What is the mass of a 15 mL sample of mercury?

Figure 6 Examples of Physical Changes

Changing from a solid to a liquid is a physical change. All changes of state are physical changes.

This aluminum can has gone through the physical change of being crushed. The properties of the can are the same.

Physical Changes Do Not Form New Substances

physical change a change of matter from one form to another without a change in chemical properties

A **physical change** is a change that affects one or more physical properties of a substance. Imagine that a piece of silver is pounded and molded into a heart-shaped pendant. This change is a physical one because only the shape of the silver has changed. The piece of silver is still silver. Its properties are the same. **Figure 6** shows more examples of physical changes.

✓ *Reading Check* What is a physical change?

Examples of Physical Changes

Freezing water to make ice cubes and sanding a piece of wood are examples of physical changes. These changes do not change the identities of the substances. Ice is still water. And sawdust is still wood. Another interesting physical change takes place when certain substances dissolve in other substances. For example, when you dissolve sugar in water, the sugar seems to disappear. But if you heat the mixture, the water evaporates. Then, you will see that the sugar is still there. The sugar went through a physical change when it dissolved.

CONNECTION TO Geology

WRITING SKILL **Erosion** Erosion of soil is a physical change. Soil erodes when wind and water move soil from one place to another. Research the history of the Grand Canyon. Write a one-page report about how erosion formed the Grand Canyon.

Matter and Physical Changes

Physical changes do not change the identity of the matter involved. A stick of butter can be melted and poured over a bowl of popcorn, as shown in **Figure 7**. Although the shape of the butter has changed, the butter is still butter, so a physical change has occurred. In the same way, if you make a figure from a lump of clay, you change the clay's shape and cause a physical change. But the identity of the clay does not change. The properties of the figure are the same as those of the lump of clay.

Figure 7 *Melting butter for popcorn involves a physical change.*

SECTION Review

Summary

- Physical properties of matter can be observed without changing the identity of the matter.
- Examples of physical properties are conductivity, state, malleability, ductility, solubility, and density.
- Density is the amount of matter in a given space.
- Density is used to identify substances because the density of a substance is always the same at a given pressure and temperature.
- When a substance undergoes a physical change, its identity stays the same.
- Examples of physical changes are freezing, cutting, bending, dissolving, and melting.

Using Key Terms

1. Use each of the following terms in a separate sentence: *physical property* and *physical change*.

Understanding Key Ideas

2. The units of density for a rectangular piece of wood are
   a. grams per milliliter.
   b. cubic centimeters.
   c. kilograms per liter.
   d. grams per cubic centimeter.

3. Explain why a golf ball is heavier than a table-tennis ball even though the balls are the same size.

4. Describe what happens to a substance when it goes through a physical change.

5. Identify six examples of physical properties.

6. List six physical changes that matter can go through.

Math Skills

7. What is the density of an object that has a mass of 350 g and a volume of 95 cm^3? Would this object float in water? Explain.

8. The density of an object is 5 g/cm^3, and the volume of the object is 10 cm^3. What is the mass of the object?

Critical Thinking

9. **Applying Concepts** How can you determine that a coin is not pure silver if you know the mass and volume of the coin?

10. **Identifying Relationships** What physical property do the following substances have in common: water, oil, mercury, and alcohol?

11. **Analyzing Processes** Explain how you would find the density of an unknown liquid if you have all of the laboratory equipment that you need.

SCILINKS

NSTA
Developed and maintained by the
National Science Teachers Association

For a variety of links related to this chapter, go to www.scilinks.org

Topic: Describing Matter; Physical Changes
SciLinks code: HSM0391; HSM1142

Chemical Properties

How would you describe a piece of wood before and after it is burned? Has it changed color? Does it have the same texture? The original piece of wood changed, and physical properties alone can't describe what happened to it.

chemical property a property of matter that describes a substance's ability to participate in chemical reactions

Chemical Properties

Physical properties are not the only properties that describe matter. **Chemical properties** describe matter based on its ability to change into new matter that has different properties. For example, when wood is burned, ash and smoke are created. These new substances have very different properties than the original piece of wood had. Wood has the chemical property of flammability. *Flammability* is the ability of a substance to burn. Ash and smoke cannot burn, so they have the chemical property of nonflammability.

Another chemical property is reactivity. *Reactivity* is the ability of two or more substances to combine and form one or more new substances. The photo of the old car in **Figure 1** illustrates reactivity and nonreactivity.

✓ **Reading Check** What does the term *reactivity* mean? (*See the Appendix for answers to Reading Checks.*)

Figure 1   **Reactivity with Oxygen**

The iron used in this old car has the chemical property of **reactivity with oxygen**. When iron is exposed to oxygen, it rusts.

The bumper on this car still looks new because it is coated with chromium. Chromium has the chemical property of **nonreactivity with oxygen.**

Figure 2 Physical Versus Chemical Properties

Physical property	Chemical property

Shape Bending an iron nail will change its shape.

Reactivity with Oxygen An iron nail can react with oxygen in the air to form iron oxide, or rust.

State Rubbing alcohol is a clear liquid at room temperature.

Flammability Rubbing alcohol is able to burn easily.

Comparing Physical and Chemical Properties

How do you tell a physical property from a chemical property? You can observe physical properties without changing the identity of the substance. For example, you can find the density and hardness of wood without changing anything about the wood.

Chemical properties, however, aren't as easy to observe. For example, you can see that wood is flammable only while it is burning. And you can observe that gold is nonflammable only when it won't burn. But a substance always has chemical properties. A piece of wood is flammable even when it's not burning. **Figure 2** shows examples of physical and chemical properties.

Characteristic Properties

The properties that are most useful in identifying a substance are *characteristic properties*. These properties are always the same no matter what size the sample is. Characteristic properties can be physical properties, such as density and solubility, as well as chemical properties, such as flammability and reactivity. Scientists rely on characteristic properties to identify and classify substances.

CONNECTION TO Social Studies

WRITING SKILL **The Right Stuff** When choosing materials to use in manufacturing, you must make sure their properties are suitable for their uses. For example, false teeth can be made from acrylic plastic, porcelain, or gold. According to legend, George Washington wore false teeth made of wood. Do research and find what Washington's false teeth were really made of. In your **science journal,** write a paragraph about what you have learned. Include information about the advantages of the materials used in modern false teeth.

Chemical Changes and New Substances

A **chemical change** happens when one or more substances are changed into new substances that have new and different properties. Chemical changes and chemical properties are not the same. Chemical properties of a substance describe which chemical changes will occur and which chemical changes will not occur. But chemical changes are the process by which substances actually change into new substances. You can learn about the chemical properties of a substance by looking at the chemical changes that take place.

You see chemical changes more often than you may think. For example, a chemical reaction happens every time a battery is used. Chemicals failing to react results in a dead battery. Chemical changes also take place within your body when the food you eat is digested. **Figure 3** describes other examples of chemical changes.

Reading Check How does a chemical change differ from a chemical property?

Figure 3 **Examples of Chemical Changes**

Soured milk smells bad because bacteria have formed new substances in the milk.

Effervescent tablets bubble when the citric acid and baking soda in them react in water.

The **hot gas** formed when hydrogen and oxygen join to make water helps blast the space shuttle into orbit.

The **Statue of Liberty** is made of orange-brown copper but it looks green from the metal's interaction with moist air. New copper compounds formed and these chemical changes made the statue turn green over time.

Figure 4 *Each of the original ingredients has different physical and chemical properties than the final product, the cake, does!*

What Happens During a Chemical Change?

A fun way to see what happens during chemical changes is to bake a cake. You combine eggs, flour, sugar, and other ingredients, as shown in **Figure 4.** When you bake the batter, you end up with something completely different. The heat of the oven and the interaction of the ingredients cause a chemical change. The result is a cake that has properties that differ from the properties of the ingredients.

Signs of Chemical Changes

Look back at **Figure 3.** In each picture, at least one sign indicates a chemical change. Other signs that indicate a chemical change include a change in color or odor, production of heat, fizzing and foaming, and sound or light being given off.

In the cake example, you would smell the cake as it baked. You would also see the batter rise and begin to brown. When you cut the finished cake, you would see the air pockets made by gas bubbles that formed in the batter. These signs show that chemical changes have happened.

Matter and Chemical Changes

Chemical changes change the identity of the matter involved. So, most of the chemical changes that occur in your daily life, such as a cake baking, would be hard to reverse. Imagine trying to unbake a cake. However, some chemical changes can be reversed by more chemical changes. For example, the water formed in the space shuttle's rockets could be split into hydrogen and oxygen by using an electric current.

chemical change a change that occurs when one or more substances change into entirely new substances with different properties

For another activity related to this chapter, go to **go.hrw.com** and type in keyword **HP5MATW.**

Figure 5 Physical and Chemical Changes

Change in Texture Grinding baking soda into a fine, powdery substance is a physical change.

Reactivity with Vinegar Gas bubbles are produced when vinegar is poured into baking soda.

Physical Versus Chemical Changes

The most important question to ask when trying to decide if a physical or chemical change has happened is, Did the composition change? The *composition* of an object is the type of matter that makes up the object and the way that the matter is arranged in the object. **Figure 5** shows both a physical and a chemical change.

A Change in Composition

Physical changes do not change the composition of a substance. For example, water is made of two hydrogen atoms and one oxygen atom. Whether water is a solid, liquid, or gas, its composition is the same. But chemical changes do alter the composition of a substance. For example, through a process called *electrolysis,* water is broken down into hydrogen and oxygen gases. The composition of water has changed, so you know that a chemical change has taken place.

Physical or Chemical Change?

1. Watch as your teacher places a burning **wooden stick** into a **test tube.** Record your observations.
2. Place a mixture of **powdered sulfur** and **iron filings** on a **sheet of paper.** Place a **bar magnet** underneath the paper, and try to separate the iron from the sulfur.
3. Drop an **effervescent tablet** into a **beaker of water.** Record your observations.
4. Identify whether each change is a physical change or a chemical change. Explain your answers.

Reversing Changes

Can physical and chemical changes be reversed? Many physical changes are easily reversed. They do not change the composition of a substance. For example, if an ice cube melts, you could freeze the liquid water to make another ice cube. But composition does change in a chemical change. So, most chemical changes are not easily reversed. Look at **Figure 6.** The chemical changes that happen when a firework explodes would be almost impossible to reverse, even if you collected all of the materials made in the chemical changes.

Figure 6 *This display of fireworks represents many chemical changes happening at the same time.*

SECTION
Review

Summary

- Chemical properties describe a substance based on its ability to change into a new substance that has different properties.

- Chemical properties can be observed only when a chemical change might happen.

- Examples of chemical properties are flammability and reactivity.

- New substances form as a result of a chemical change.

- Unlike a chemical change, a physical change does not alter the identity of a substance.

Using Key Terms

1. In your own words, write a definition for each of the following terms: *chemical property* and *chemical change*.

Understanding Key Ideas

2. Rusting is an example of a
   a. physical property.
   b. physical change.
   c. chemical property.
   d. chemical change.

3. Which of the following is a characteristic property?
   a. density
   b. chemical reactivity
   c. solubility in water
   d. All of the above

4. Write two examples of chemical properties and explain what they are.

5. The Statue of Liberty was originally a copper color. After being exposed to the air, she turned a greenish color. What kind of change happened? Explain your answer.

6. Explain how to tell the difference between a physical and a chemical property.

Math Skills

7. The temperature of an acid solution is 25°C. A strip of magnesium is added, and the temperature rises 2°C each minute for the first 3 min. After another 5 min, the temperature has risen two more degrees. What is the final temperature?

Critical Thinking

8. **Making Comparisons** Describe the difference between physical and chemical changes in terms of what happens to the matter involved in each kind of change.

9. **Applying Concepts** Identify two physical properties and two chemical properties of a bag of microwave popcorn before popping and after.

Skills Practice Lab

White Before Your Eyes

You have learned how to describe matter based on its physical and chemical properties. You have also learned some signs that can help you determine whether a change in matter is a physical change or a chemical change. In this lab, you'll use what you have learned to describe four substances based on their properties and the changes that they undergo.

Procedure

1 Copy Table 1 and Table 2 shown on the next page. Be sure to leave plenty of room in each box to write down your observations.

2 Using a spatula, place a small amount of baking powder into three cups of your egg carton. Use just enough baking powder to cover the bottom of each cup. Record your observations about the baking powder's appearance, such as color and texture, in the "Unmixed" column of Table 1.

③ Use an eyedropper to add 60 drops of water to the baking powder in the first cup. Stir with the stirring rod. Record your observations in Table 1 in the column labeled "Mixed with water." Clean your stirring rod.

④ Use a clean dropper to add 20 drops of vinegar to the second cup of baking powder. Stir. Record your observations in Table 1 in the column labeled "Mixed with vinegar." Clean your stirring rod.

⑤ Use a clean dropper to add five drops of iodine solution to the third cup of baking powder. Stir. Record your observations in Table 1 in the column labeled "Mixed with iodine solution." Clean your stirring rod. **Caution:** Be careful when using iodine. Iodine will stain your skin and clothes.

⑥ Repeat steps 2–5 for each of the other substances (baking soda, cornstarch, and sugar). Use a clean spatula for each substance.

Analyze the Results

① **Examining Data** What physical properties do all four substances share?

② **Analyzing Data** In Table 2, write the type of change—physical or chemical—that you observed for each substance. State the property that the change demonstrates.

Draw Conclusions

③ **Evaluating Results** Classify the four substances by the chemical property of reactivity. For example, which substances are reactive with vinegar (acid)?

Table 1 Observations				
Substance	**Unmixed**	**Mixed with water**	**Mixed with vinegar**	**Mixed with iodine solution**
Baking powder				
Baking soda				
Cornstarch				
Sugar				

Table 2 Changes and Properties						
	Mixed with water		**Mixed with vinegar**		**Mixed with iodine solution**	
Substance	**Change**	**Property**	**Change**	**Property**	**Change**	**Property**
Baking powder						
Baking soda						
Cornstarch						
Sugar						

Chapter Review

1 Use each of the following terms in a separate sentence: *physical property, chemical property, physical change,* and *chemical change.*

For each pair of terms, explain how the meanings of the terms differ.

2 *mass* and *weight*

3 *inertia* and *mass*

4 *volume* and *density*

UNDERSTANDING KEY IDEAS

Multiple Choice

5 Which of the following properties is NOT a chemical property?

a. reactivity with oxygen

b. malleability

c. flammability

d. reactivity with acid

6 The volume of a liquid can be expressed in all of the following units EXCEPT

a. grams.

b. liters.

c. milliliters.

d. cubic centimeters.

7 The SI unit for the mass of a substance is the

a. gram.

b. liter.

c. milliliter.

d. kilogram.

8 The best way to measure the volume of an irregularly shaped solid is to

a. use a ruler to measure the length of each side of the object.

b. weigh the solid on a balance.

c. use the water displacement method.

d. use a spring scale.

9 Which of the following statements about weight is true?

a. Weight is a measure of the gravitational force on an object.

b. Weight varies depending on where the object is located in relation to the Earth.

c. Weight is measured by using a spring scale.

d. All of the above

10 Which of the following statements does NOT describe a physical property of a piece of chalk?

a. Chalk is a solid.

b. Chalk can be broken into pieces.

c. Chalk is white.

d. Chalk will bubble in vinegar.

11 Which of the following statements about density is true?

a. Density is expressed in grams.

b. Density is mass per unit volume.

c. Density is expressed in milliliters.

d. Density is a chemical property.

Short Answer

12 In one or two sentences, explain how the process of measuring the volume of a liquid differs from the process of measuring the volume of a solid.

13 What is the formula for calculating density?

14 List three characteristic properties of matter.

Math Skills

15 What is the volume of a book that has a width of 10 cm, a length that is 2 times the width, and a height that is half the width? Remember to express your answer in cubic units.

16 A jar contains 30 mL of glycerin (whose mass is 37.8 g) and 60 mL of corn syrup (whose mass is 82.8 g). Which liquid is on top? Show your work, and explain your answer.

CRITICAL THINKING

17 **Concept Mapping** Use the following terms to create a concept map: *matter, mass, inertia, volume, milliliters, cubic centimeters, weight,* and *gravity.*

18 **Applying Concepts** Develop a set of questions that would be useful when identifying an unknown substance. The substance may be a liquid, a gas, or a solid.

19 **Analyzing Processes** You are making breakfast for your friend Filbert. When you take the scrambled eggs to the table, he asks, "Would you please poach these eggs instead?" What scientific reason do you give Filbert for not changing his eggs?

20 **Identifying Relationships** You look out your bedroom window and see your new neighbor moving in. Your neighbor bends over to pick up a small cardboard box, but he cannot lift it. What can you conclude about the item(s) in the box? Use the terms *mass* and *inertia* to explain how you came to your conclusion.

21 **Analyzing Ideas** You may sometimes hear on the radio or on TV that astronauts are weightless in space. Explain why this statement is not true.

INTERPRETING GRAPHICS

Use the photograph below to answer the questions that follow.

22 List three physical properties of this aluminum can.

23 When this can was crushed, did it undergo a physical change or a chemical change?

24 How does the density of the metal in the crushed can compare with the density of the metal before the can was crushed?

25 Can you tell what the chemical properties of the can are by looking at the picture? Explain your answer.

Standardized Test Preparation

Read each of the passages below. Then, answer the questions that follow each passage.

Passage 1 Astronomers were studying the motions of galaxies in space when they noticed something odd. They thought that the large gravitational force, which causes the galaxies to rotate rapidly, was due to a large amount of mass in the galaxies. Then, they discovered that the mass of the galaxies was not great enough to explain this large gravitational force. So, what was causing the additional gravitational force? One theory is that the universe contains matter that we cannot see with our eyes or our telescopes. Astronomers call this invisible matter <u>dark matter</u>.

1. According to this passage, what did astronomers originally think caused the rotation of the galaxies?
   A a lack of inertia
   B a large gravitational force
   C a small amount of mass in the galaxies
   D a small gravitational force

2. Why do you think astronomers use the term *dark matter*?
   F Dark matter refers to dark objects.
   G Dark matter refers to matter that we can't see.
   H You need a telescope to see dark matter.
   I All large objects are dark.

3. Which statement is the best summary of the passage?
   A The enormous amount of mass in the galaxies explains why the galaxies rotate.
   B Dark matter may be responsible for the gravitational force that causes the rotation of galaxies.
   C Invisible matter is called dark matter.
   D Galaxies rotate as they move through the universe.

Passage 2 Blimps and dirigibles are types of airships. An airship consists of an engine, a large balloon that contains gas, and a gondola that carries passengers and crew. Airships float in air because the gases that the airships contain are less dense than air. In the early 1900s, airships were commonly used for travel, including transatlantic flights. Airships were less frequently used after the 1937 explosion and crash of the *Hindenburg* in New Jersey. The *Hindenburg* was filled with <u>flammable</u> hydrogen gas instead of helium gas, which is nonflammable.

1. In this passage, what does *flammable* mean?
   A able to burn
   B able to float
   C able to sink
   D not able to burn

2. Which of the following statements is true according to the passage?
   F Hydrogen gas is nonflammable.
   G Airships float because they contain gases that are less dense than air.
   H Helium gas was used in the *Hindenburg*.
   I The gondola contains gas.

3. Which of the following statements about airships is true?
   A Airships are still a major mode of transportation.
   B Airships now contain nonflammable, hydrogen gas.
   C Airships consist of an engine, a gondola, and a large balloon.
   D Airships traveled only in the United States.

The table below shows the properties of different substances. Use the table below to answer the questions that follow.

Properties of Some Substances*		
Substance	State	Density (g/cm³)
Helium	Gas	0.0001663
Pyrite	Solid	5.02
Mercury	Liquid	13.55
Gold	Solid	19.32

* at room temperature and pressure

1. What could you use to tell pyrite (fool's gold) and gold apart?

  A volume

  B density

  C mass

  D state

2. What do you think would happen if you placed a nugget of pyrite into a beaker of mercury?

  F The pyrite would sink.

  G The pyrite would dissolve.

  H The mercury and the pyrite would react.

  I The pyrite would float.

3. If a nugget of pyrite and a nugget of gold each have a mass of 50 g, what can you conclude about the volume of each nugget?

  A The volume of pyrite is greater than the volume of gold.

  B The volume of pyrite is less than the volume of gold.

  C The volumes of the substances are equal.

  D There is not enough information to determine the answer.

4. Which substance has the **lowest** density?

  F helium

  G pyrite

  H mercury

  I gold

Read each question below, and choose the best answer.

1. Imagine that you have discovered a new element, and you want to find its density. It has a mass of 78.8 g and a volume of 8 cm³. To find the density of the element, you must divide the element's mass by its volume. What is the density of the element?

  A 0.102 g/cm³

  B 0.98 g/cm³

  C 9.85 g/cm³

  D 630.4 g/cm³

2. Many soft drinks come in bottles that contain about 590 mL. If the density of a soft drink is 1.05 g/mL, what is the mass of the drink?

  F 0.0018 g

  G 498.2 g

  H 561.9 g

  I 619.5 g

3. If you have 150 g of pure gold and the density of gold is 19.32 g/cm³, what is the volume of your gold nugget?

  A 2,898 cm³

  B 7.76 cm³

  C 0.98 cm³

  D 0.13 cm³

4. Three objects have a mass of 16 g each. But their volumes differ. Object A, a liquid, has a volume of 1.2 mL. Object B, a solid, has a volume of 3.2 cm³. Object C, another solid, has a volume of 1.9 cm³. Which object is the least dense?

  F object A

  G object B

  H object C

  I There is not enough information to determine the answer.

Standardized Test Preparation

Science in Action

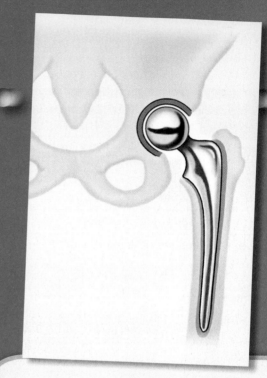

Scientific Debate

Paper or Plastic?

What do you choose at the grocery store: paper or plastic bags? Plastic bags are waterproof and take up less space. You can use them to line waste cans and to pack lunches. Some places will recycle plastic bags. But making 1 ton of plastic bags uses 11 barrels of oil, which can't be replaced, and produces polluting chemicals. On the other hand, making 1 ton of paper bags destroys 13 to 17 trees, which take years to replace. Paper bags, too, can be reused for lining waste cans and wrapping packages. Recycling paper pollutes less than recycling plastic does. What is the answer? Maybe we should reuse both!

Language Arts ACTiViTY

WRITING SKILL There are advantages and disadvantages of each kind of bag. Write a one-page essay defending your position on this subject. Support your opinion with facts.

Science, Technology, and Society

Building a Better Body

Have you ever broken a bone? If so, you probably wore a cast while the bone healed. But what happens if the bone is too damaged to heal? Sometimes, a false bone made from titanium can replace the damaged bone. Titanium appears to be a great bone-replacement material. It is a lightweight but strong metal. It can attach to existing bone and resists chemical changes. But, friction can wear away titanium bones. Research has found that implanting a form of nitrogen on the titanium makes the metal last longer.

Social Studies ACTiViTY

Do some research on the history of bone-replacement therapy. Make a poster that shows a timeline of events leading up to current technology.

Mimi So

Gemologist and Jewelry Designer A typical day for gemologist and jewelry designer Mimi So involves deciding what materials to work with. When she chooses a gemstone for a piece of jewelry, she must consider the size, hardness, color, grade, and cut of the stone. When choosing a metal to use as a setting for a stone, she must look at the hardness, melting point, color, and malleability of the metal. She needs to choose a metal that not only looks good with a particular stone but also has physical properties that will work with that stone. For example, Mimi So says emeralds are soft and fragile. A platinum setting would be too hard and could damage the emerald. So, emeralds are usually set in a softer metal, such as 18-karat gold.

The chemical properties of stones must also be considered. Heating can burn or discolor some gemstones. Mimi So says, "If you are using pearls in a design that requires heating the metal, the pearl is not a stone, so you cannot heat the pearl, because it would destroy the pearl."

Math ACTIVITY

Pure gold is 24-karat (24K). Gold that contains 18 parts gold and 6 parts other metals is 18-karat gold. The percentage of gold in 18K gold is found by dividing the amount of gold by the total amount of the material and then multiplying by 100%. For example, (18 parts gold)/(24 parts total) equals $0.75 \times 100\% = 75\%$ gold. Find the percentage of gold in 10K and 14K gold.

To learn more about these Science in Action topics, visit **go.hrw.com** and type in the keyword **HP5MATF**.

Current Science

Check out Current Science® articles related to this chapter by visiting go.hrw.com. Just type in the keyword HP5CS02.

2

States of Matter

The Big Idea

Matter exists in various physical states, which are determined by the movement of the matter's particles.

About the PHOTO

This beautiful glass creation by artist Dale Chihuly is entitled "Mille Fiori" (A Thousand Flowers). The pieces that form the sculpture were not always solid and unchanging. Each individual piece started as a blob of melted glass on the end of a hollow pipe. The artist worked with his assistants to quickly form each shape before the molten glass cooled and became a solid again.

PRE-READING ACTIVITY

FOLDNOTES **Three-Panel Flip Chart**
Before you read the chapter, create the FoldNote entitled "Three-Panel Flip Chart" described in the **Study Skills** section of the Appendix. Label the flaps of the three-panel flip chart with "Solid," "Liquid," and "Gas." As you read the chapter, write information you learn about each category under the appropriate flap.

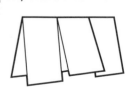

START-UP ACTIVITY

Vanishing Act

In this activity, you will use isopropyl alcohol (rubbing alcohol) to investigate a change of state.

Procedure

1. Pour **rubbing alcohol** into a **small plastic cup** until the alcohol just covers the bottom of the cup.

2. Moisten the tip of a **cotton swab** by dipping it into the alcohol in the cup.

3. Rub the cotton swab on the palm of your hand. Make sure there are no cuts or abrasions on your hands.

4. Record your observations.

5. Wash your hands thoroughly.

Analysis

1. Explain what happened to the alcohol after you rubbed the swab on your hand.

2. Did you feel a sensation of hot or cold? If so, how do you explain what you observed?

3. Record your answers.

Three States of Matter

You've just walked home on one of the coldest days of the year. A fire is blazing in the fireplace. And there is a pot of water on the stove to make hot chocolate.

The water begins to bubble. Steam rises from the pot. You make your hot chocolate, but it is too hot to drink. You don't want to wait for it to cool down. So, you add an ice cube. You watch the ice melt in the hot liquid until the drink is at just the right temperature. Then, you enjoy your hot drink while warming yourself by the fire.

The scene described above has examples of the three most familiar states of matter: solid, liquid, and gas. The **states of matter** are the physical forms in which a substance can exist. For example, water commonly exists in three states of matter: solid (ice), liquid (water), and gas (steam).

Particles of Matter

Matter is made up of tiny particles called *atoms* and *molecules* (MAHL i kyoolz). These particles are too small to see without a very powerful microscope. Atoms and molecules are always in motion and are always bumping into one another. The particles interact with each other, and the way they interact with each other helps determine the state of the matter. **Figure 1** describes three states of matter—solid, liquid, and gas—in terms of the speed and attraction of the particles.

What You Will Learn

● Describe the properties shared by particles of all matter.
● Describe three states of matter.
● Explain the differences between the states of matter.

Vocabulary

states of matter
solid
liquid
surface tension
viscosity
gas

READING STRATEGY

Paired Summarizing Read this section silently. In pairs, take turns summarizing the material. Stop to discuss ideas that seem confusing.

Figure 1 Models of a Solid, a Liquid, and a Gas

Particles of a solid do not move fast enough to overcome the strong attraction between them. So, they are close together and vibrate in place.

Particles of a liquid move fast enough to overcome some of the attraction between them. The particles are close together but can slide past one another.

Particles of a gas move fast enough to overcome almost all of the attraction between them. The particles are far apart and move independently of one another.

Solids

Imagine dropping a marble into a bottle. Would anything happen to the shape or size of the marble? Would the shape or size of the marble change if you put it in a larger bottle?

Solids Have Definite Shape and Volume

Even in a bottle, a marble keeps its original shape and volume. The marble's shape and volume stay the same no matter what size bottle you drop it into because the marble is a solid. A **solid** is the state of matter that has a definite shape and volume.

The particles of a substance in a solid state are very close together. The attraction between them is stronger than the attraction between the particles of the same substance in the liquid or gaseous state. The particles in a solid move, but they do not move fast enough to overcome the attraction between them. Each particle vibrates in place. Therefore, each particle is locked in place by the particles around it.

There Are Two Kinds of Solids

There are two kinds of solids—*crystalline* (KRIS tuhl in) and *amorphous* (uh MAWR fuhs). Crystalline solids have a very orderly, three-dimensional arrangement of particles. The particles of crystalline solids are in a repeating pattern of rows. Iron, diamond, and ice are examples of crystalline solids.

Amorphous solids are made of particles that do not have a special arrangement. So, each particle is in one place, but the particles are not arranged in a pattern. Examples of amorphous solids are glass, rubber, and wax. **Figure 2** shows a photo of quartz (a crystalline solid) and glass (an amorphous solid).

✓ **Reading Check** How are the particles in a crystalline solid arranged? (*See the Appendix for answers to Reading Checks.*)

states of matter the physical forms of matter, which include solid, liquid, and gas

solid the state of matter in which the volume and shape of a substance are fixed

CONNECTION TO Physics

Is Glass a Liquid? At one time, there was a theory that glass was a liquid. This theory came about because of the observation that ancient windowpanes were often thicker at the bottom than at the top. People thought that the glass had flowed to the bottom of the pane, so glass must be a liquid. Research this theory. Present your research to your class in an oral presentation.

ACTIVITY

Figure 2 Crystalline and Amorphous Solids

The particles of crystalline solids, such as this quartz crystal, have an orderly three-dimensional pattern.

Glass, an amorphous solid, is made of particles that are not arranged in any particular pattern.

Figure 3 *Although their shapes are different, the beaker and the graduated cylinder each contain 350 mL of juice.*

Liquids

What do you think would change about orange juice if you poured the juice from a can into a glass? Would the volume of juice be different? Would the taste of the juice change?

Liquids Change Shape but Not Volume

The only thing that would change when the juice is poured into the glass is the shape of the juice. The shape changes because juice is a liquid. **Liquid** is the state of matter that has a definite volume but takes the shape of its container. The particles in liquids move fast enough to overcome some of the attractions between them. The particles slide past each other until the liquid takes the shape of its container.

Although liquids change shape, they do not easily change volume. A can of juice contains a certain volume of liquid. That volume stays the same if you pour the juice into a large container or a small one. **Figure 3** shows the same volume of liquid in two different containers.

Liquids Have Unique Characteristics

A special property of liquids is surface tension. **Surface tension** is a force that acts on the particles at the surface of a liquid. Surface tension causes some liquids to form spherical drops, like the beads of water shown in **Figure 4.** Different liquids have different surface tensions. For example, gasoline has a very low surface tension and forms flat drops.

Another important property of liquids is viscosity. **Viscosity** is a liquid's resistance to flow. Usually, the stronger the attractions between the molecules of a liquid, the more viscous the liquid is. For example, honey flows more slowly than water. So, honey has a higher viscosity than water.

✓ Reading Check What is viscosity?

liquid the state of matter that has a definite volume but not a definite shape

surface tension the force that acts on the surface of a liquid and that tends to minimize the area of the surface

viscosity the resistance of a gas or liquid to flow

gas a form of matter that does not have a definite volume or shape

Figure 4 *Water forms spherical drops as a result of surface tension.*

Gases

Would you believe that one small tank of helium can fill almost 700 balloons? How is this possible? After all, the volume of a tank is equal to the volume of only about five filled balloons. The answer has to do with helium's state of matter.

Gases Change in Both Shape and Volume

Helium is a gas. **Gas** is the state of matter that has no definite shape or volume. The particles of a gas move quickly. So, they can break away completely from one another. There is less attraction between particles of a gas than between particles of the same substance in the solid or liquid state.

The amount of empty space between gas particles can change. Look at **Figure 5.** The particles of helium in the balloons are farther apart than the particles of helium in the tank. The particles spread out as helium fills the balloon. So, the amount of empty space between the gas particles increases.

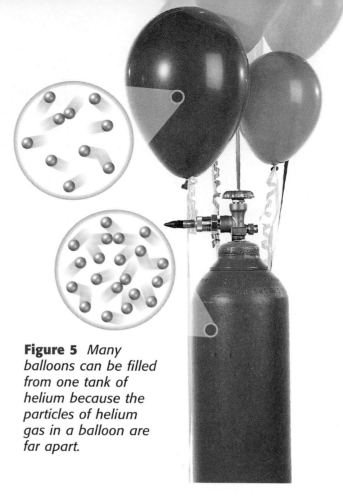

Figure 5 *Many balloons can be filled from one tank of helium because the particles of helium gas in a balloon are far apart.*

SECTION Review

Summary

- The three most familiar states of matter are solid, liquid, and gas.
- All matter is made of tiny particles called atoms and molecules that attract each other and move constantly.
- A solid has a definite shape and volume.
- A liquid has a definite volume but not a definite shape.
- A gas does not have a definite shape or volume.

Using Key Terms

1. Use each of the following terms in a separate sentence: *viscosity* and *surface tension*.

Understanding Key Ideas

2. One property that all particles of matter have in common is they

   a. never move in solids.

   b. only move in gases.

   c. move constantly.

   d. None of the above

3. Describe solids, liquids, and gases in terms of shape and volume.

Critical Thinking

4. **Applying Concepts** Classify each substance according to its state of matter: apple juice, bread, a textbook, and steam.

5. **Identifying Relationships** The volume of a gas can change, but the volume of a solid cannot. Explain why this is true.

Interpreting Graphics

Use the image below to answer the questions that follow.

6. Identify the state of matter shown in the jar.

7. Discuss how the particles in the jar are attracted to each other.

Developed and maintained by the
National Science Teachers Association

For a variety of links related to this chapter, go to www.scilinks.org

Topic: Solids, Liquids, and Gases
SciLinks code: HSM1420

Behavior of Gases

Suppose you are watching a parade that you have been looking forward to for weeks. You may be fascinated by the giant balloons floating high overhead.

You may wonder how the balloons were arranged for the parade. How much helium was needed to fill all of the balloons? What role does the weather play in getting the balloons to float?

Describing Gas Behavior

Helium is a gas. Gases behave differently from solids or liquids. Unlike the particles that make up solids and liquids, gas particles have a large amount of empty space between them. The space that gas particles occupy is the gas's volume, which can change because of temperature and pressure.

Temperature

How much helium is needed to fill a parade balloon, like the one in **Figure 1?** The answer depends on the outdoor temperature. **Temperature** is a measure of how fast the particles in an object are moving. The faster the particles are moving, the more energy they have. So, on a hot day, the particles of gas are moving faster and hitting the inside walls of the balloon harder. Thus, the gas is expanding and pushing on the walls of the balloon with greater force. If the gas expands too much, the balloon will explode. But, what will happen if the weather is cool on the day of the parade? The particles of gas in the balloon will have less energy. And, the particles of gas will not push as hard on the walls of the balloon. So, more gas must be used to fill the balloons.

What You Will Learn

- Describe three factors that affect how gases behave.
- Predict how a change in pressure or temperature will affect the volume of a gas.

Vocabulary

temperature
volume
pressure
Boyle's Law
Charles's Law

READING STRATEGY

Reading Organizer As you read this section, make a table comparing the effects of temperature, volume, and pressure on gases.

temperature a measure of how hot (or cold) something is; specifically, a measure of the movement of particles.

Figure 1 *To properly inflate a helium balloon, you must consider the temperature outside of the balloon.*

Volume

Volume is the amount of space that an object takes up. But because the particles of a gas spread out, the volume of any gas depends on the container that the gas is in. For example, have you seen inflated balloons that were twisted into different shapes? Shaping the balloons was possible because particles of gas can be compressed, or squeezed together, into a smaller volume. But, if you tried to shape a balloon filled with water, the balloon would probably explode. It would explode because particles of liquids can't be compressed as much as particles of gases.

Pressure

The amount of force exerted on a given area of surface is called **pressure.** You can think of pressure as the number of times the particles of a gas hit the inside of their container.

The balls in **Figure 2** are the same size, which means they can hold the same volume of air, which is a gas. Notice, however, that there are more particles of gas in the basketball than in the beach ball. So, more particles hit the inside surface of the basketball than hit the inside surface of the beach ball. When more particles hit the inside surface of the basketball, the force on the inside surface of the ball increases. This increased force leads to greater pressure, which makes the basketball feel harder than the beach ball.

✓ **Reading Check** **Why is the pressure greater in a basketball than in a beach ball?** (*See the Appendix for answers to Reading Checks*.)

volume a measure of the size of a body or region in three-dimensional space

pressure the amount of force exerted per unit area of a surface

INTERNET ACTIVITY

For another activity related to this chapter, go to **go.hrw.com** and type in the keyword **HP5STAW**.

Figure 2 Gas and Pressure

High pressure

Low pressure

The basketball has a higher pressure because there are more particles of gas in it, and they are closer together. The particles collide with the inside of the ball at a faster rate.

The beach ball has a lower pressure because there are fewer particles of gas, and they are farther apart. The particles in the beach ball collide with the inside of the ball at a slower rate.

Gas Behavior Laws

Scientists found that the temperature, pressure, and volume of a gas are linked. Changing one of the factors changes the other two factors. The relationships between temperature, pressure, and volume are described by gas laws.

Boyle's Law

Imagine that a diver 10 m below the surface of a lake blows a bubble of air. When the bubble reaches the surface, the bubble's volume has doubled. The difference in pressure between the surface and 10 m below the surface caused this change.

The relationship between the volume and pressure of a gas was first described by Robert Boyle, a 17th-century Irish chemist. The relationship is now known as Boyle's law. **Boyle's law** states that for a fixed amount of gas at a constant temperature, the volume of the gas is inversely related to the pressure. So, as the pressure of a gas increases, the volume decreases by the same amount, as shown in **Figure 3.**

Charles's Law

If you blow air into a balloon and leave it in the hot sun, the balloon might pop. **Charles's law** states that for a fixed amount of gas at a constant pressure, the volume of the gas changes in the same way that the temperature of the gas changes. So, if the temperature increases, the volume of gas also increases by the same amount. Charles's law is shown by the model in **Figure 4.**

✓ Reading Check State Charles's law in your own words.

Boyle's law the law that states that the volume of a gas is inversely proportional to the pressure of a gas when temperature is constant

Charles's law the law that states that the volume of a gas is directly proportional to the temperature of a gas when pressure is constant

Figure 3 Boyle's Law

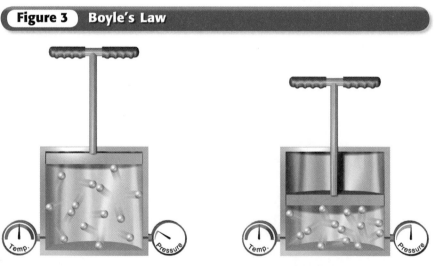

Lifting the piston lets the particles of gas spread far apart. The volume of the gas increases as the pressure decreases.

Releasing the piston allows the particles of gas to return to their original volume and pressure.

Pushing the piston forces the gas particles close together. The volume of the gas decreases as the pressure increases.

Figure 4 **Charles's Law**

Decreasing the temperature of the gas causes the particles to move more slowly. The gas particles hit the piston less often and with less force. So, the volume of the gas decreases.

Increasing the temperature of the gas causes the particles to move more quickly. The gas particles hit the piston more often and with greater force. So, the volume of the gas increases.

SECTION
Review

Summary

- Temperature measures how fast the particles in an object are moving.

- Gas pressure increases as the number of collisions of gas particles increases.

- Boyle's law states that if the temperature doesn't change, the volume of a gas increases as the pressure decreases.

- Charles's law states that if the pressure doesn't change, the volume of a gas increases as the temperature increases.

Using Key Terms

1. Use each of the following terms in the same sentence: *temperature, pressure, volume,* and *Charles's law.*

Understanding Key Ideas

2. Boyle's law describes the relationship between
   a. volume and pressure.
   b. temperature and pressure.
   c. temperature and volume.
   d. All of the above

3. What are the effects of a warm temperature on gas particles?

Math Skills

4. You have 3 L of gas at a certain temperature and pressure. What would the volume of the gas be if the temperature doubled and the pressure stayed the same?

Critical Thinking

5. **Applying Concepts** What happens to the volume of a balloon that is taken outside on a cold winter day? Explain.

6. **Making Inferences** When scientists record a gas's volume, they also record its temperature and pressure. Why?

7. **Analyzing Ideas** What happens to the pressure of a gas if the volume of gas is tripled at a constant temperature?

Changes of State

It can be tricky to eat a frozen juice bar outside on a hot day. In just minutes, the juice bar will start to melt. Soon the solid juice bar becomes a liquid mess.

As the juice bar melts, it goes through a change of state. In this section, you will learn about the four changes of state shown in **Figure 1** as well as a fifth change of state called *sublimation* (SUHB luh MAY shuhn).

Energy and Changes of State

A **change of state** is the change of a substance from one physical form to another. All changes of state are physical changes. In a physical change, the identity of a substance does not change. In **Figure 1,** the ice, liquid water, and steam are all the same substance—water.

The particles of a substance move differently depending on the state of the substance. The particles also have different amounts of energy when the substance is in different states. For example, particles in liquid water have more energy than particles in ice. But particles of steam have more energy than particles in liquid water. So, to change a substance from one state to another, you must add or remove energy.

✓ **Reading Check** What is a change of state? (*See the Appendix for answers to Reading Checks.*)

What You Will Learn

- Describe how energy is involved in changes of state.
- Describe what happens during melting and freezing.
- Compare evaporation and condensation.
- Explain what happens during sublimation.
- Identify the two changes that can happen when a substance loses or gains energy.

Vocabulary

change of state
melting
evaporation
boiling
condensation
sublimation

READING STRATEGY

Mnemonics As you read this section, create a mnemonic device to help you remember the five changes of state.

change of state the change of a substance from one physical state to another

Figure 1 Changes of State

The terms in the arrows are changes of state. Water commonly goes through the changes of state shown here.

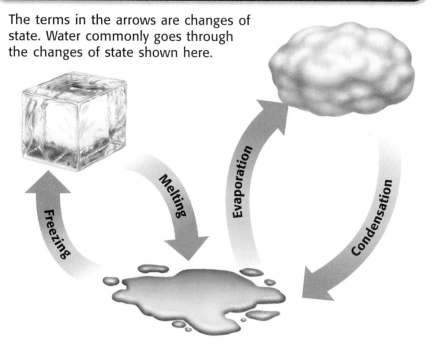

Melting: Solid to Liquid

One change of state that happens when you add energy to a substance is melting. **Melting** is the change of state from a solid to a liquid. This change of state is what happens when ice melts. Adding energy to a solid increases the temperature of the solid. As the temperature increases, the particles of the solid move faster. When a certain temperature is reached, the solid will melt. The temperature at which a substance changes from a solid to a liquid is the *melting point* of the substance. Melting point is a physical property. Different substances have different melting points. For example, gallium melts at about 30°C. Because your normal body temperature is about 37°C, gallium will melt in your hand! This is shown in **Figure 2.** Table salt, however, has a melting point of 801°C, so it will not melt in your hand.

Figure 2 *Even though gallium is a metal, it would not be very useful as jewelry!*

Adding Energy

For a solid to melt, particles must overcome some of their attractions to each other. When a solid is at its melting point, any energy added to it is used to overcome the attractions that hold the particles in place. Melting is an *endothermic* (EN doh THUHR mik) change because energy is gained by the substance as it changes state.

melting the change of state in which a solid becomes a liquid by adding energy

Freezing: Liquid to Solid

The change of state from a liquid to a solid is called *freezing*. The temperature at which a liquid changes into a solid is the liquid's *freezing point*. Freezing is the reverse process of melting. Thus, freezing and melting occur at the same temperature, as shown in **Figure 3.**

Removing Energy

For a liquid to freeze, the attractions between the particles must overcome the motion of the particles. Imagine that a liquid is at its freezing point. Removing energy will cause the particles to begin locking into place. Freezing is an *exothermic* (EK so THUHR mik) change because energy is removed from the substance as it changes state.

Figure 3 *Liquid water freezes at the same temperature at which ice melts—0°C.*

If energy is added at 0°C, the ice will melt.

If energy is removed at 0°C, the liquid water will freeze.

Evaporation: Liquid to Gas

One way to experience evaporation is to iron a shirt using a steam iron. You will notice steam coming up from the iron as the wrinkles disappear. This steam forms when the liquid water in the iron becomes hot and changes to gas.

Boiling and Evaporation

Evaporation (ee VAP uh RAY shuhn) is the change of a substance from a liquid to a gas. Evaporation can occur at the surface of a liquid that is below its boiling point. For example, when you sweat, your body is cooled through evaporation. Your sweat is mostly water. Water absorbs energy from your skin as the water evaporates. You feel cooler because your body transfers energy to the water. Evaporation also explains why water in a glass on a table disappears after several days.

Figure 4 explains the difference between boiling and evaporation. **Boiling** is the change of a liquid to a vapor, or gas, throughout the liquid. Boiling occurs when the pressure inside the bubbles, which is called *vapor pressure*, equals the outside pressure on the bubbles, or atmospheric pressure. The temperature at which a liquid boils is called its *boiling point*. No matter how much of a substance is present, neither the boiling point nor the melting point of a substance change. For example, 5 mL and 5 L of water both boil at 100°C.

Reading Check What is evaporation?

evaporation the change of a substance from a liquid to a gas

boiling the conversion of a liquid to a vapor when the vapor pressure of the liquid equals the atmospheric pressure

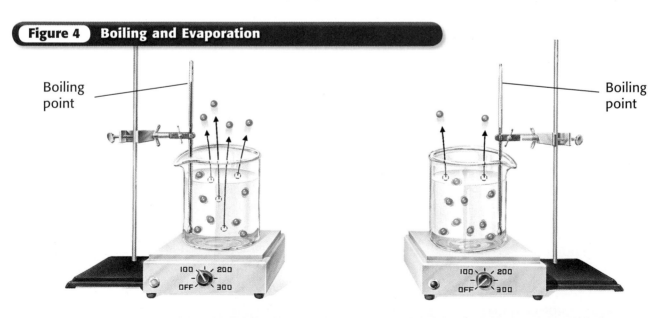

Figure 4 Boiling and Evaporation

Boiling point

Boiling point

Boiling occurs in a liquid at its boiling point. As energy is added to the liquid, particles throughout the liquid move faster. When they move fast enough to break away from other particles, they evaporate and become a gas.

Evaporation can also occur in a liquid below its boiling point. Some particles at the surface of the liquid move fast enough to break away from the particles around them and become a gas.

Effects of Pressure on Boiling Point

Earlier, you learned that water boils at 100°C. In fact, water boils at 100°C only at sea level, because of atmospheric pressure. Atmospheric pressure is caused by the weight of the gases that make up the atmosphere.

Atmospheric pressure varies depending on where you are in relation to sea level. Atmospheric pressure is lower at higher elevations. The higher you go above sea level, the fewer air particles there are above you. So, the atmospheric pressure is lower. Imagine boiling water at the top of a mountain. The boiling point would be lower than 100°C. For example, Denver, Colorado, is 1.6 km above sea level. In Denver, water boils at about 95°C.

Condensation: Gas to Liquid

Look at the dragonfly in **Figure 5.** Notice the beads of water that have formed on the wings. They form because of condensation of gaseous water in the air. **Condensation** is the change of state from a gas to a liquid. Condensation and evaporation are the reverse of each other. The *condensation point* of a substance is the temperature at which the gas becomes a liquid. And the condensation point is the same temperature as the boiling point at a given pressure.

For a gas to become a liquid, large numbers of particles must clump together. Particles clump together when the attraction between them overcomes their motion. For this to happen, energy must be removed from the gas to slow the movement of the particles. Because energy is removed, condensation is an exothermic change.

CONNECTION TO Language Arts

WRITING SKILL Cooking at High Altitudes Many times, cake mixes and other prepared foods will have special instructions for baking and cooking at high altitudes. Even poaching an egg at a high altitude requires a different amount of cooking time. Imagine that you got a letter from a cousin in Denver. He is upset that a cake he made turned out poorly, even though he followed the recipe. Do research on cooking at high altitudes. Write a letter to your cousin explaining why he may have had problems baking the cake.

condensation the change of state from a gas to a liquid

Figure 5 *Beads of water form when water vapor in the air contacts a cool surface, such as the wings of this dragonfly.*

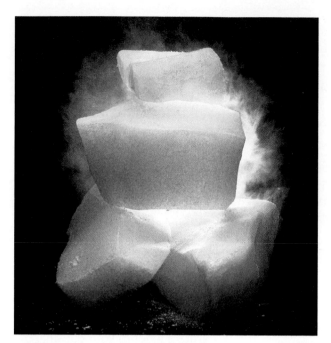

Figure 6 *Dry ice changes directly from a solid to a gas. This change of state is called* sublimation.

sublimation the process in which a solid changes directly into a gas

Sublimation: Solid to Gas

The solid in **Figure 6** is dry ice. Dry ice is carbon dioxide in a solid state. It is called *dry ice* because instead of melting into a liquid, it goes through sublimation. **Sublimation** is the change of state in which a solid changes directly into a gas. Dry ice is much colder than ice made from water.

For a solid to change directly into a gas, the particles of the substance must move from being very tightly packed to being spread far apart. So, the attractions between the particles must be completely overcome. The substance must gain energy for the particles to overcome their attractions. Thus, sublimation is an endothermic change because energy is gained by the substance as it changes state.

Change of Temperature Vs. Change of State

When most substances lose or gain energy, one of two things happens to the substance: its temperature changes or its state changes. The temperature of a substance is related to the speed of the substance's particles. So, when the temperature of a substance changes, the speed of the particles also changes. But the temperature of a substance does not change until the change of state is complete. For example, the temperature of boiling water stays at 100°C until it has all evaporated. In **Figure 7,** you can see what happens to ice as energy is added to the ice.

✓ Reading Check What happens to the temperature of a substance as it changes state?

Boiling Water Is Cool

1. Remove the cap from a **syringe**.
2. Place the tip of the syringe in the **warm water** that is provided by your teacher. Pull the plunger out until you have 10 mL of water in the syringe.
3. Tighten the cap on the syringe.
4. Hold the syringe, and slowly pull the plunger out.
5. Observe any changes you see in the water. Record your observations.
6. Why are you not burned by the water in the syringe?

Figure 7 **Changing the State of Water**

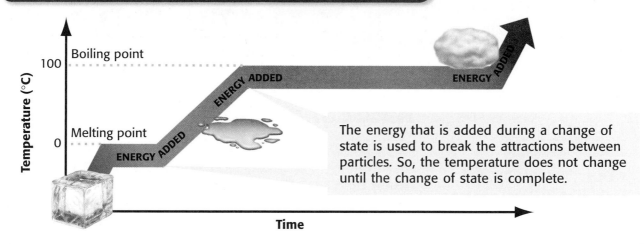

The energy that is added during a change of state is used to break the attractions between particles. So, the temperature does not change until the change of state is complete.

SECTION
Review

Summary

- A change of state is the conversion of a substance from one physical form to another.

- Energy is added during endothermic changes. Energy is removed during exothermic changes.

- The freezing point and the melting point of a substance are the same temperature.

- Both boiling and evaporation result in a liquid changing to a gas.

- Condensation is the change of a gas to a liquid. It is the reverse of evaporation.

- Sublimation changes a solid directly to a gas.

- The temperature of a substance does not change during a change of state.

Using Key Terms

For each pair of terms, explain how the meanings of the terms differ.

1. *melting* and *freezing*

2. *condensation* and *evaporation*

Understanding Key Ideas

3. The change from a solid directly to a gas is called

   a. evaporation.

   b. boiling.

   c. melting.

   d. sublimation.

4. Describe how the motion and arrangement of particles in a substance change as the substance freezes.

5. Explain what happens to the temperature of an ice cube as it melts.

6. How are evaporation and boiling different? How are they similar?

Math Skills

7. The volume of a substance in the gaseous state is about 1,000 times the volume of the same substance in the liquid state. How much space would 18 mL of water take up if it evaporated?

Critical Thinking

8. **Evaluating Data** The temperature of water in a beaker is 25°C. After adding a piece of magnesium to the water, the temperature increases to 28°C. Is this an exothermic or endothermic reaction? Explain your answer.

9. **Applying Concepts** Solid crystals of iodine were placed in a flask. The top of the flask was covered with aluminum foil. The flask was gently heated. Soon, the flask was filled with a reddish gas. What change of state took place? Explain your answer.

10. **Predicting Consequences** Would using dry ice in your holiday punch cause it to become watery after several hours? Why or why not?

Skills Practice Lab

A Hot and Cool Lab

When you add energy to a substance through heating, does the substance's temperature always go up? When you remove energy from a substance through cooling, does the substance's temperature always go down? In this lab you'll investigate these important questions with a very common substance—water.

Procedure

1 Fill the beaker about one-third to one-half full with water.

2 Put on heat-resistant gloves. Turn on the hot plate, and put the beaker on it. Put the thermometer in the beaker. **Caution:** Be careful not to touch the hot plate.

3 Make a copy of Table I. Record the temperature of the water every 30 seconds. Continue doing this until about one-fourth of the water boils away. Note the first temperature reading at which the water is steadily boiling.

Table 1								
Time (s)	30	60	90	120	150	180	210	etc.
Temperature (ºC)		DO NOT		WRITE IN		BOOK		

4 Turn off the hot plate.

5 While the beaker is cooling, make a graph of temperature (*y*-axis) versus time (*x*-axis). Draw an arrow pointing to the first temperature at which the water was steadily boiling.

OBJECTIVES

Measure and record time and temperature accurately.

Graph the temperature change of water as it changes state.

Analyze and interpret graphs of changes of state.

MATERIALS

- beaker, 250 or 400 mL
- coffee can, large
- gloves, heat-resistant
- graduated cylinder, 100 mL
- graph paper
- hot plate
- ice, crushed
- rock salt
- stopwatch
- thermometer
- water
- wire-loop stirring device

SAFETY

6 After you finish the graph, use heat-resistant gloves to pick up the beaker. Pour the warm water out, and rinse the warm beaker with cool water.
Caution: Even after cooling, the beaker is still too warm to handle without gloves.

7 Put approximately 20 mL of water in the graduated cylinder.

8 Put the graduated cylinder in the coffee can, and fill in around the graduated cylinder with crushed ice. Pour rock salt on the ice around the graduated cylinder. Place the thermometer and the wire-loop stirring device in the graduated cylinder.

9 As the ice melts and mixes with the rock salt, the level of ice will decrease. Add ice and rock salt to the can as needed.

10 Make another copy of Table I. Record the temperature of the water in the graduated cylinder every 30 seconds. Stir the water with the stirring device.
Caution: Do not stir with the thermometer.

11 Once the water begins to freeze, stop stirring. Do not try to pull the thermometer out of the solid ice in the cylinder.

12 Note the temperature when you first notice ice crystals forming in the water. Continue taking readings until the water in the graduated cylinder is completely frozen.

13 Make a graph of temperature (*y*-axis) versus time (*x*-axis). Draw an arrow to the temperature reading at which the first ice crystals form in the water in the graduated cylinder.

Analyze the Results

1 **Describing Events** What happens to the temperature of boiling water when you continue to add energy through heating?

2 **Describing Events** What happens to the temperature of freezing water when you continue to remove energy through cooling?

3 **Analyzing Data** What does the slope of each graph represent?

4 **Analyzing Results** How does the slope of the graph that shows water boiling compare with the slope of the graph before the water starts to boil? Why is the slope different for the two periods?

5 **Analyzing Results** How does the slope of the graph showing water freezing compare with the slope of the graph before the water starts to freeze? Why is the slope different for the two periods?

Draw Conclusions

6 **Evaluating Data** The particles that make up solids, liquids, and gases are in constant motion. Adding or removing energy causes changes in the movement of these particles. Using this idea, explain why the temperature graphs of the two experiments look the way they do.

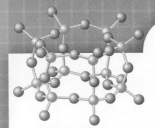

Chapter Review

USING KEY TERMS

For each pair of terms, explain how the meanings of the terms differ.

1 *solid* and *liquid*

2 *Boyle's law* and *Charles's law*

3 *evaporation* and *boiling*

4 *condensation* and *sublimation*

UNDERSTANDING KEY IDEAS

Multiple Choice

5 Which of the following statements best describes the particles of a liquid?

  a. The particles are far apart and moving fast.

  b. The particles are close together but moving past each other.

  c. The particles are far apart and moving slowly.

  d. The particles are closely packed and vibrating in place.

6 Which of the following statements describes what happens as the temperature of a gas in a balloon increases?

  a. The speed of the particles decreases.

  b. The volume of the gas increases, and the speed of the particles increases.

  c. The volume of the gas decreases.

  d. The pressure of the gas decreases.

7 Boiling points and freezing points are examples of

  a. chemical properties. **c.** energy.

  b. physical properties. **d.** matter.

8 Dew collecting on a spider web in the early morning is an example of

  a. condensation. **c.** sublimation.

  b. evaporation. **d.** melting.

9 During which change of state do atoms or molecules become more ordered?

  a. boiling **c.** melting

  b. condensation **d.** sublimation

10 Which of the following changes of state is exothermic?

  a. evaporation **c.** freezing

  b. melting **d.** All of the above

11 What happens to the volume of a gas inside a cylinder if the temperature does not change but the pressure is reduced?

  a. The volume of the gas increases.

  b. The volume of the gas stays the same.

  c. The volume of the gas decreases.

  d. There is not enough information to determine the answer.

12 The atoms and molecules in matter

  a. are attracted to one another.

  b. are constantly moving.

  c. move faster at higher temperatures.

  d. All of the above

Short Answer

13 Explain why liquid water takes the shape of its container but an ice cube does not.

14 Rank solids, liquids, and gases in order of particle speed from the highest speed to the lowest speed.

Math Skills

15 Kate placed 100 mL of water in five different pans, placed the pans on a windowsill for a week, and measured how much water evaporated from each pan. Draw a graph of her data, which is shown below. Place surface area on the x-axis and volume evaporated on the y-axis. Is the graph linear or non-linear? What does this information tell you?

Pan number	1	2	3	4	5
Surface area (cm²)	44	82	20	30	65
Volume evaporated (mL)	42	79	19	29	62

CRITICAL THINKING

16 Concept Mapping Use the following terms to create a concept map: *states of matter, solid, liquid, gas, changes of state, freezing, evaporation, condensation,* and *melting.*

17 Analyzing Ideas In the photo below, water is being split to form two new substances, hydrogen and oxygen. Is this a change of state? Explain your answer.

18 Applying Concepts After taking a shower, you notice that small droplets of water cover the mirror. Explain how this happens. Be sure to describe where the water comes from and the changes it goes through.

19 Analyzing Methods To protect their crops during freezing temperatures, orange growers spray water onto the trees and allow it to freeze. In terms of energy lost and energy gained, explain why this practice protects the oranges from damage.

20 Making Inferences At sea level, water boils at 100°C, while methane boils at –161°C. Which of these substances has a stronger force of attraction between its particles? Explain your reasoning.

INTERPRETING GRAPHICS

Use the graph below to answer the questions that follow.

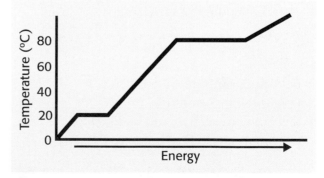

21 What is the boiling point of the substance? What is the melting point?

22 Which state is present at 30°C?

23 How will the substance change if energy is added to the liquid at 20°C?

Standardized Test Preparation

Read each of the passages below. Then, answer the questions that follow each passage.

Passage 1 Did you know that lightning can turn sand into glass? If lightning strikes sand, the sand can reach temperatures of up to 33,000°C. That temperature is as hot as the surface of the sun! This <u>intense</u> heat melts the sand into a liquid. The liquid quickly cools and hardens into glass. This glass is a rare and beautiful type of natural glass called *fulgurite*.

The same basic process is used to make light bulbs, windows, and bottles. But instead of lightning, glassmakers use hot ovens to melt solid silica (the main ingredient of sand) and other ingredients into liquid glass. Then, before the glass cools and solidifies, the glassmaker forms the glass into the desired shape.

1. In the glassmaking process, what happens after the glassmaker forms the material into the desired shape?

  A Solid silica melts in a hot oven.

  B Solid silica is struck by lightning.

  C The glass melts and becomes a liquid.

  D The glass cools and solidifies.

2. Which statement is an opinion from the passage?

  F Lightning can form fulgurites.

  G Fulgurites are beautiful.

  H Lightning heats the sand to 33,000°C.

  I Glassmakers use very hot ovens.

3. In the passage, what does *intense* mean?

  A a small amount

  B gaseous

  C a great amount

  D causing something to melt

Passage 2 For thousands of years, people used wind, water, gravity, dogs, horses, and cattle to do work. But until about 300 years ago, people had little success finding other things to help them do work. Then in 1690, Denis Papin, a French mathematician and physicist, noticed that steam <u>expanding</u> in a cylinder pushed a piston up. As the steam then cooled and contracted, the piston fell. Watching the motion of the piston, Papin had an idea. He connected a water-pump handle to the piston. As the pump handle rose and fell with the piston, water was pumped.

Throughout the next hundred years, other scientists and inventors improved upon Papin's design. In 1764, James Watt turned the steam pump into a true steam engine that could drive a locomotive. Watt's engine helped start the Industrial Revolution.

1. In the passage, what does *expanding* mean?

  A enlarging

  B enhancing

  C enforcing

  D disappearing

2. According to the passage, how was steam used?

  F as a source of power for thousands of years

  G by Denis Papin only in France

  H to pump water in the late 1600s

  I in the steam engine first

3. Which of the following statements is a fact from the passage?

  A Steam expands and causes a piston to fall.

  B When steam cools, it expands.

  C The invention of the water pump started the Industrial Revolution.

  D People began using steam as a source of power 300 years ago.

Use the chart below to answer the questions that follow.

Freezing Points of 50:50 Mixtures of Antifreeze and Water

Brand	Freezing Point (°C)
Ice-B-Gone	−5
Freeze Free	−7
Liqui-Freeze	−9
Auntie Freeze	−11

1. Phillip wants to purchase antifreeze for his car. Antifreeze is added to the water in a car's radiator to lower the water's freezing point. The temperature in his area never falls below −10°C. Given the information in the chart above, which of the following brands of antifreeze would be the best for Phillip's car?

   A Ice-B-Gone
   B Freeze-Free
   C Liqui-Freeze
   D Auntie Freeze

2. Phillip wants to make a bar graph that compares the brands of antifreeze. If he puts the brand name of each antifreeze on the *x*-axis, what variable belongs on the *y*-axis?

   F Freezing point of water
   G Freezing point of water with antifreeze in it
   H Freezing point of the antifreeze only
   I Freezing point of the radiator

3. Phillip's cousin lives in an area where it rarely freezes. The record low temperature for winter is −2°C. Which brand should Phillip's cousin purchase?

   A Ice-B-Gone
   B Freeze-Free
   C Liqui-Freeze
   D Auntie Freeze

Read each question below, and choose the best answer.

1. Gerard and three of his friends each want to buy a kite. The kites regularly cost $7.95, but they are on sale for $4.50. How much will their total savings be if they all purchase their kites on sale?

   A $13.80
   B $18.00
   C $10.35
   D $23.85

2. Francis bought a 2 L bottle of juice. How many milliliters of juice does this bottle hold?

   F 0.002 mL
   G 0.2 mL
   H 200 mL
   I 2,000 mL

3. Which of the following lists contains ratios that are all equivalent to 3/4?

   A 3/4, 6/8, 15/22
   B 6/10, 15/20, 20/25
   C 3/4, 15/20, 20/25
   D 3/4, 6/8, 15/20

4. The Liu family went to the state fair in their home state. They purchased five tickets, which cost $6.50 each. Tickets for the rides cost $1.25 each, and all five family members rode six rides. Two daughters bought souvenirs that cost $5.25 each. Snacks cost a total of $12.00. What is the total amount of money the family spent on their outing?

   F $61.25
   G $140.50
   H $62.50
   I $92.50

Science in Action

Science, Technology, and Society

Deep-sea Diving with Helium

Divers who breathe air while deep in the ocean run the risk of suffering from nitrogen narcosis. Nitrogen narcosis produces an alcohol-like effect, which can cause a diver to become disoriented and to use poor judgment. This toxic effect can lead to dangerous behavior. To avoid nitrogen narcosis, divers who work at depths of more than 60 m breathe heliox. *Heliox* is a mixture of helium and oxygen, instead of air. The main disadvantage of heliox is that helium conducts heat about six times faster than nitrogen does, so a diver using heliox will feel cold sooner than a diver who is breathing air.

Math ACTiViTY

There are 2.54 centimeters in one inch. How many feet deep could a diver go before he or she started experiencing nitrogen narcosis?

Scientific Discoveries

The Fourth State of Matter

If you heat water, it will eventually turn into a gas. But what would happen if you kept on heating the gas? Scientists only had to look to the sun for the answer. The sun, like other stars, is made of the fourth state of matter—plasma. Plasma is a superheated gas. Once a gas's temperature rises above 10,000°C to 20,000°C, its particles start to break apart and it becomes plasma. Unlike gas, plasma can create, and be affected by, electrical and magnetic fields. More than 99% of the known universe is made of plasma! Even Earth has some naturally occurring plasma. Plasma can be found in auroras, flames, and lightning.

Social Studies ACTiViTY

Research plasma. Find out how plasma is used in today's technology, such as plasma TVs. How will this new technology affect you and society in general? Describe your findings in a poster.

Andy Goldsworthy

Nature Artist Most of the art that Andy Goldsworthy creates will melt, decay, evaporate, or just blow away. He uses leaves, water, sticks, rocks, ice, and snow to create art. Goldsworthy observes how nature works and how it changes over time, and uses what he learns to create his art. For example, on cold, sunny mornings, Goldsworthy makes frost shadows. He stands with his back to the sun, which creates a shadow on the ground. The rising sun warms the ground and melts the frost around his shadow. When he steps away, he can see the shape of his body in the frost that is left on the ground.

In his art, Goldsworthy sometimes shows water in the process of changing states. For example, he made huge snowballs filled with branches, pebbles, and flowers. He then stored these snowballs in a freezer until summer, when they were displayed in a museum. As they melted, the snowballs slowly revealed their contents. Goldsworthy says his art reflects nature, because nature is constantly changing. Fortunately, he takes pictures of his art so we can enjoy it even after it disappears!

Language Arts ACTiViTY

WRITING SKILL Research Andy Goldsworthy's art. Write a one-page review of one of his creations. Be sure to include what you like or don't like about the art.

go.hrw.com
To learn more about these Science in Action topics, visit **go.hrw.com** and type in the keyword **HP5STAF.**

Current Science
Check out Current Science® articles related to this chapter by visiting go.hrw.com. Just type in the keyword **HP5CS03.**

3

Elements, Compounds, and Mixtures

The Big Idea

Matter can be classified into elements, compounds, and mixtures.

About the

Within these liquid-filled glass lamps, colored globs slowly rise and fall. But what are these liquids, and what keeps them from mixing together? The liquid inside these lamps is a mixture. This mixture is composed of four compounds, which include mineral oil, wax, water, and alcohol. The water and alcohol mix, but they remain separated from the globs of wax and oil.

PRE-READING ACTiViTY

FOLDNOTES **Key-Term Fold** Before you read the chapter, create the FoldNote entitled "Key-Term Fold" described in the **Study Skills** section of the Appendix. Write a key term from the chapter on each tab of the key-term fold. Under each tab, write the definition of the key term.

Mystery Mixture

In this activity, you will separate the different dyes found in an ink mixture.

Procedure

1. Place a **pencil** on top of a **clear plastic cup.** Tear a strip of paper (3 cm × 15 cm) from a **coffee filter.** Wrap one end of the strip around a pencil so that the other end will touch the bottom of the plastic cup. Use **tape** to attach the paper to the pencil.

2. Take the paper out of the cup. Using a **water-soluble black marker,** make a small dot in the center of the strip about 2 cm from the bottom.

3. Pour **water** in the cup to a depth of 1 cm. Lower the paper into the cup. Keep the dot above water.

4. Remove the paper when the water is 1 cm from the top. Record your observations.

Analysis

1. What happened as the paper soaked up the water?

2. Which colors make up the marker's black ink?

3. Compare your results with those of your classmates. Record your observations.

4. Is the process used to make the ink separate a physical or a chemical change? Explain.

Elements

Imagine that you work for the Break-It-Down Company. Your job is to break down materials into simpler substances.

You haven't had any trouble breaking down materials so far. But one rainy Monday morning, you get a material that seems very hard to break down. First, you try physical changes, such as crushing and melting. But these do not change the material into something simpler. Next, you try some chemical changes, such as passing an electric current through the material. These do not change it either. What's going on?

What You Will Learn

- Describe pure substances.
- Describe the characteristics of elements, and give examples.
- Explain how elements can be identified.
- Classify elements according to their properties.

Vocabulary

element
pure substance
metal
nonmetal
metalloid

READING STRATEGY

Reading Organizer As you read this section, make a concept map by using the terms above.

Elements, the Simplest Substances

You couldn't break down the material described above because it is an element. An **element** is a pure substance that cannot be separated into simpler substances by physical or chemical means. In this section, you'll learn about elements and the properties that help you classify them.

Only One Type of Particle

Elements are pure substances. A **pure substance** is a substance in which there is only one type of particle. So, each element contains only one type of particle. These particles, called *atoms*, are much too small for us to see. For example, every atom in a 5 g nugget of the element gold is like every other atom of gold. The particles of a pure substance are alike no matter where they are found, as shown in **Figure 1.**

✓**Reading Check** Explain why an element is a pure substance. (*See the Appendix for answers to Reading Checks.*)

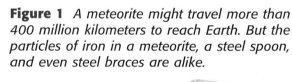

Figure 1 *A meteorite might travel more than 400 million kilometers to reach Earth. But the particles of iron in a meteorite, a steel spoon, and even steel braces are alike.*

Properties of Elements

Each element can be identified by its unique set of properties. For example, each element has its own *characteristic properties*. These properties do not depend on the amount of the element present. Characteristic properties include some physical properties, such as boiling point, melting point, and density. Chemical properties, such as reactivity with acid, are also characteristic properties.

An element may share a property with another element, but other properties can help you tell the elements apart. For example, the elements helium and krypton are both unreactive gases. However, the densities (mass per unit volume) of these elements are different. Helium is less dense than air. A helium-filled balloon will float up if it is released. Krypton is denser than air. A krypton-filled balloon will sink to the ground if it is released.

Identifying Elements by Their Properties

Look at the elements shown in **Figure 2.** These three elements have some similar properties. But each element can be identified by its unique set of properties.

Notice that the physical properties shown in **Figure 2** include melting point and density. Other physical properties, such as color, hardness, and texture, could be added to the list. Chemical properties might also be useful. For example, some elements, such as hydrogen and carbon, are flammable. Other elements, such as sodium, react with oxygen at room temperature. Still other elements, including zinc, are reactive with acid.

Separating Elements

1. Examine a sample of nails provided by your teacher.

2. Your sample has **aluminum nails** and **iron nails.** Try to separate the two kinds of nails. Group similar nails into piles.

3. Pass a **bar magnet** over each pile of nails. Record your results.

4. Were you successful in completely separating the two types of nails? Explain.

5. Based on your observations, explain how the properties of aluminum and iron could be used to separate cans in a recycling plant.

element a substance that cannot be separated or broken down into simpler substances by chemical means

pure substance a sample of matter, either a single element or a single compound, that has definite chemical and physical properties

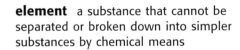

Figure 2 **The Unique Properties of Elements**

Cobalt

- Melting point: 1,495°C
- Density: 8.9 g/cm^3
- Conducts electric current and heat energy
- Unreactive with oxygen in the air

Iron

- Melting point: 1,535°C
- Density: 7.9 g/cm^3
- Conducts electric current and heat energy
- Combines slowly with oxygen in the air to form rust

Nickel

- Melting point: 1,455°C
- Density: 8.9 g/cm^3
- Conducts electric current and heat energy
- Unreactive with oxygen in the air

Figure 3 *Even though these dogs are different breeds, they have enough in common to be classified as terriers.*

Classifying Elements by Their Properties

Think about how many different breeds of dogs there are. Now, think about how you tell one breed from another. Most often, you can tell just by their appearance, or the physical properties, of the dogs. **Figure 3** shows several breeds of terriers. Many terriers are fairly small in size and have short hair. Not all terriers are alike, but they share enough properties to be classified in the same group.

Categories of Elements

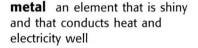

metal an element that is shiny and that conducts heat and electricity well

nonmetal an element that conducts heat and electricity poorly

metalloid an element that has properties of both metals and nonmetals

Elements are also grouped into categories by the properties they share. There are three major categories of elements: metals, nonmetals, and metalloids. The elements iron, nickel, and cobalt are all metals. Not all metals are exactly alike, but they do have some properties in common. **Metals** are shiny, and they conduct heat energy and electric current. **Nonmetals** make up the second category of elements. They do not conduct heat or electric current, and solid nonmetals are dull in appearance. **Metalloids,** which have properties of both metals and nonmetals, make up the last category.

✔ **Reading Check** What are three characteristics of metals?

Categories Are Similar

Imagine being in a music store. The CDs are categorized by type of music. If you like rock-and-roll, you would go to the rock-and-roll section. You might not know every CD, but you know that a CD has the characteristics of rock-and-roll for it to be in this section.

By knowing the category to which an unfamiliar element belongs, you can predict some of its properties. **Figure 4** shows examples of each category and describes the properties that identify elements in each category.

Figure 4 **The Three Major Categories of Elements**

Metals

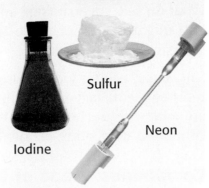

Lead
Tin
Copper

Metals are elements that are shiny and are good conductors of heat and electric current. They are *malleable.* (They can be hammered into thin sheets.) They are also *ductile.* (They can be drawn into thin wires.)

Nonmetals

Sulfur
Iodine
Neon

Nonmetals are elements that are dull (not shiny) and that are poor conductors of heat and electric current. Solids tend to be brittle and unmalleable. Few familiar objects are made of only nonmetals.

Metalloids

Boron
Silicon
Antimony

Metalloids are also called semiconductors. They have properties of both metals and nonmetals. Some metalloids are shiny. Some are dull. Metalloids are somewhat malleable and ductile. Some metalloids conduct heat and electric current as well.

SECTION Review

Summary

- A substance in which all of the particles are alike is a pure substance.

- An element is a pure substance that cannot be broken down into anything simpler by physical or chemical means.

- Each element has a unique set of physical and chemical properties.

- Elements are classified as metals, nonmetals, or metalloids, based on their properties.

Using Key Terms

1. Use the following terms in the same sentence: *element* and *pure substance.*

Understanding Key Ideas

2. A metalloid
   a. may conduct electric current.
   b. can be ductile.
   c. is also called a semiconductor.
   d. All of the above

3. What is a pure substance?

Math Skills

4. There are eight elements that make up 98.5% of the Earth's crust: 46.6% oxygen, 8.1% aluminum, 5.0% iron, 3.6% calcium, 2.8% sodium, 2.6% potassium, and 2.1% magnesium. The rest is silicon. What percentage of the Earth's crust is silicon?

Critical Thinking

5. **Applying Concepts** From which category of elements would you choose to make a container that wouldn't shatter if dropped? Explain your answer.

6. **Making Comparisons** Compare the properties of metals, nonmetals, and metalloids.

7. **Evaluating Assumptions** Your friend tells you that a shiny element has to be a metal. Do you agree? Explain.

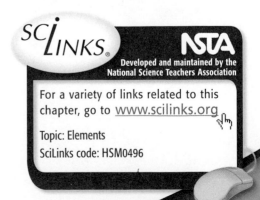

SCiLINKS®

NSTA
Developed and maintained by the
National Science Teachers Association

For a variety of links related to this chapter, go to www.scilinks.org

Topic: Elements
SciLinks code: HSM0496

Compounds

What do salt, sugar, baking soda, and water have in common? You might use all of these to bake bread. Is there anything else similar about them?

Salt, sugar, baking soda, and water are all compounds. Because most elements take part in chemical changes fairly easily, they are rarely found alone in nature. Instead, they are found combined with other elements as compounds.

Compounds: Made of Elements

A **compound** is a pure substance composed of two or more elements that are chemically combined. Elements combine by reacting, or undergoing a chemical change, with one another. A particle of a compound is a molecule. Molecules of compounds are formed when atoms of two or more elements join together.

In **Figure 1,** you see magnesium reacting with oxygen. A compound called *magnesium oxide* is forming. The compound is a new pure substance. It is different from the elements that make it up. Most of the substances that you see every day are compounds. **Table 1** lists some familiar examples.

The Ratio of Elements in a Compound

Elements do not randomly join to form compounds. Elements join in a specific ratio according to their masses to form a compound. For example, the ratio of the mass of hydrogen to the mass of oxygen in water is 1 to 8. This mass ratio can be written as 1:8. This ratio is always the same. Every sample of water has a 1:8 mass ratio of hydrogen to oxygen. What happens if a sample of a compound has a different mass ratio of hydrogen to oxygen? The compound cannot be water.

What You Will Learn

- Explain how elements make up compounds.
- Describe the properties of compounds.
- Explain how a compound can be broken down into its elements.
- Give examples of common compounds.

Vocabulary

compound

READING STRATEGY

Prediction Guide Before reading this section, write the title of each heading in this section. Next, under each heading, write what you think you will learn.

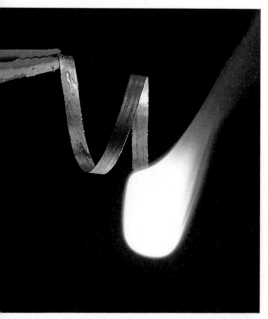

Figure 1 *As magnesium burns, it reacts with oxygen and forms the compound magnesium oxide.*

Table 1 Familiar Compounds	
Compound	**Elements combined**
Table salt	sodium and chlorine
Water	hydrogen and oxygen
Vinegar	hydrogen, carbon, and oxygen
Carbon dioxide	carbon and oxygen
Baking soda	sodium, hydrogen, carbon, and oxygen

Quick Lab

Compound Confusion

1. Measure **4 g of compound A,** and place it in a **clear plastic cup.**

2. Measure **4 g of compound B**, and place it in a **second clear plastic cup.**

3. Observe the color and texture of each compound. Record your observations.

4. Add **5 mL of vinegar** to each cup. Record your observations.

5. Baking soda reacts with vinegar. Powdered sugar does not react with vinegar. Which compound is baking soda, and which compound is powdered sugar? Explain your answer.

Properties of Compounds

As an element does, each compound has its own physical properties. Physical properties include melting point, density, and color. Compounds can also be identified by their different chemical properties. Some compounds react with acid. For example, calcium carbonate, found in chalk, reacts with acid. Other compounds, such as hydrogen peroxide, react when exposed to light.

compound a substance made up of atoms of two or more different elements joined by chemical bonds

✓ **Reading Check** What are three physical properties used to identify compounds? (*See the Appendix for answers to Reading Checks.*)

Properties: Compounds Versus Elements

A compound has properties that differ from those of the elements that form it. Look at **Figure 2.** Sodium chloride, or table salt, is made of two very dangerous elements—sodium and chlorine. Sodium reacts violently with water. Chlorine is a poisonous gas. But when combined, these elements form a harmless compound with unique properties. Sodium chloride is safe to eat. It also dissolves (without exploding!) in water.

Figure 2   Forming Sodium Chloride

Sodium is a soft, silvery white metal that reacts violently with water.

Chlorine is a poisonous, greenish yellow gas.

Sodium chloride, or table salt, is a white solid. It dissolves easily in water and is safe to eat.

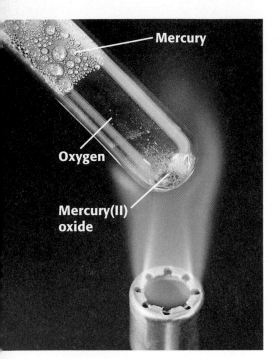

Mercury

Oxygen

Mercury(II)
oxide

Figure 3 *Heating mercury(II) oxide causes a chemical change that separates it into the elements mercury and oxygen.*

Breaking Down Compounds

Some compounds can be broken down into their elements by chemical changes. Other compounds break down to form simpler compounds instead of elements. These simpler compounds can then be broken down into elements through more chemical changes. For example, carbonic acid is a compound that helps give carbonated beverages their "fizz." When you open a carbonated beverage, carbonic acid breaks down into carbon dioxide and water. Carbon dioxide and water can then be broken down into the elements carbon, oxygen, and hydrogen through chemical changes.

✓ Reading Check Compounds can be broken down into what two types of substances?

Methods of Breaking Down Compounds

The only way to break down a compound is through a chemical change. Sometimes, energy is needed for a chemical change to happen. Two ways to add energy to break down a compound are to apply heat and to apply an electric current. For example, heating the compound mercury(II) oxide breaks it down into the elements mercury and oxygen, as shown in **Figure 3.**

Compounds in Your World

You are surrounded by compounds. Compounds make up the food you eat, the school supplies you use, and the clothes you wear—even you!

Compounds in Industry

The compounds found in nature are not usually the raw materials needed by industry. Often, these compounds must be broken down to provide elements or other compounds that can be used as raw material. For example, aluminum is used in cans and airplanes. But aluminum is not found alone in nature. Aluminum is produced by breaking down the compound aluminum oxide. Ammonia is another important compound used in industry. It is used to make fertilizers. Ammonia is made by combining the elements nitrogen and hydrogen.

INTERNET ACTIVITY

For another activity related to this chapter, go to **go.hrw.com** and type in the keyword **HP5MIXW.**

CONNECTION TO Physics

Electrolysis The process of using electric current to break down compounds is known as *electrolysis*. For example, electrolysis can be used to separate water into hydrogen and oxygen. Research ways that electrolysis is used in industry. Make a poster of what you learn, and present a report to your class.

ACTIVITY

Compounds in Nature

Proteins are compounds found in all living things. The element nitrogen is one of the elements needed to make proteins. **Figure 4** shows how some plants get the nitrogen they need. Other plants use nitrogen compounds that are in the soil. Animals get the nitrogen they need by eating plants or by eating animals that have eaten plants. The proteins in the food are broken down as an animal digests the food. The simpler compounds that form are used by the animal's cells to make new proteins.

Another compound that plays an important role in life is carbon dioxide. You exhale carbon dioxide that was made in your body. Plants take in carbon dioxide, which is used in photosynthesis. Plants use photosynthesis to make compounds called carbohydrates. These carbohydrates can then be broken down for energy through other chemical changes by plants or animals.

Figure 4 *The bumps on the roots of this pea plant are home to bacteria that form compounds from nitrogen in the air. The pea plant makes proteins from these compounds.*

SECTION Review

Summary

- A compound is a pure substance composed of two or more elements.
- The elements that form a compound always combine in a specific ratio according to their masses.
- Each compound has a unique set of physical and chemical properties that differ from those of the elements that make up the compound.
- Compounds can be broken down into simpler substances only by chemical changes.

Using Key Terms

1. In your own words, write a definition for the term *compound*.

Understanding Key Ideas

2. The elements in a compound
   a. join in a specific ratio according to their masses.
   b. combine by reacting with one another.
   c. can be separated by chemical changes.
   d. All of the above

3. What type of change is needed to break down a compound?

Math Skills

4. Table sugar is a compound made of carbon, hydrogen, and oxygen. If sugar contains 41.86% carbon and 6.98% hydrogen, what percentage of sugar is oxygen?

Critical Thinking

5. **Applying Concepts** Iron is a solid, gray metal. Oxygen is a colorless gas. When they chemically combine, rust is made. Rust has a reddish brown color. Why is rust different from the iron and oxygen that it is made of?

6. **Analyzing Ideas** A jar contains samples of the elements carbon and oxygen. Does the jar contain a compound? Explain your answer.

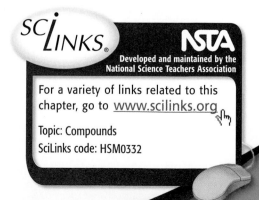

SCiLINKS

NSTA
Developed and maintained by the
National Science Teachers Association

For a variety of links related to this chapter, go to www.scilinks.org

Topic: Compounds
SciLinks code: HSM0332

Mixtures

Imagine that you roll out some dough, add tomato sauce, and sprinkle some cheese on top. Then, you add green peppers, mushrooms, olives, and pepperoni! What have you just made?

A pizza, of course! But that's not all. You have also created a mixture—and a delicious one at that! In this section, you will learn about mixtures and their properties.

Properties of Mixtures

All mixtures—even pizza—share certain properties. A **mixture** is a combination of two or more substances that are not chemically combined. When two or more materials are put together, they form a mixture if they do not react to form a compound. For example, cheese and tomato sauce do not react when they are used to make a pizza. So, a pizza is a mixture.

No Chemical Changes in a Mixture

No chemical change happens when a mixture is made. So, each substance in a mixture has the same chemical makeup it had before the mixture formed. That is, each substance in a mixture keeps its identity. In some mixtures, such as the pizza in **Figure 1,** you can see each of the components. In other mixtures, such as salt water, you cannot see all the components.

✓ Reading Check Why do substances in a mixture keep their identities? (*See the Appendix for answers to Reading Checks.*)

Separating Mixtures Through Physical Methods

You don't like mushrooms on your pizza? Just pick them off. This change is a physical change of the mixture. The identities of the substances do not change. But not all mixtures are as easy to separate as a pizza. You cannot just pick salt out of a saltwater mixture. One way to separate the salt from the water is to heat the mixture until the water evaporates. The salt is left behind. Other ways to separate mixtures are shown in **Figure 2.**

What You Will Learn

● Describe three properties of mixtures.
● Describe four methods of separating the parts of a mixture.
● Analyze a solution in terms of its solute and solvent.
● Explain how concentration affects a solution.
● Describe the particles in a suspension.
● Explain how a colloid differs from a solution and a suspension.

Vocabulary

mixture	concentration
solution	solubility
solute	suspension
solvent	colloid

READING STRATEGY

Reading Organizer As you read this section, create an outline of the section. Use the headings from the section in your outline.

mixture a combination of two or more substances that are not chemically combined

Figure 1 *You can see each topping on this mixture, which is better known as a pizza.*

Figure 2   Common Ways to Separate Mixtures

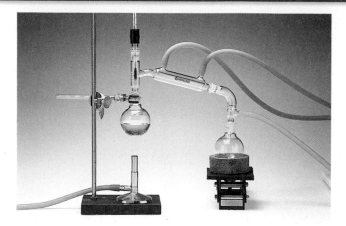

Distillation (DIS tuh LAY shuhn) is a process that separates a mixture based on the boiling points of the components. Here, pure water (at right) is being distilled from a salt-water mixture (at left). Distillation is also used to separate crude oil into components, such as gasoline and kerosene.

A **magnet** can be used to separate a mixture of the elements iron and aluminum. Iron is attracted to the magnet, but aluminum is not.

The different parts of blood are separated using a machine called a **centrifuge** (SEN truh FYOOJ). In the test tube at left, a layer of plasma rests above a layer of red blood cells. A centrifuge separates mixtures by the densities of the components.

Separating a mixture of sodium chloride (table salt) and sulfur takes more than one step.

❶ In the first step, water is added, and the mixture is stirred. Salt dissolves in water. Sulfur does not.

❷ In the second step, the mixture is poured through a filter. The filter traps the solid sulfur.

❸ In the third step, the water is evaporated. The sodium chloride is left behind.

Table 1 Mixtures and Compounds	
Mixtures	**Compounds**
Made of elements, compounds, or both	Made of elements
No change in original properties of components	Change in original properties of components
Separated by physical means	Separated by chemical means
Formed using any ratio of components	Formed using a set ratio of components

The Ratio of Components in a Mixture

A compound is made of elements in a specific mass ratio. However, the components of a mixture do not need to be mixed in a definite ratio. For example, granite is a mixture made of three minerals: feldspar, mica, and quartz. Feldspar is pink in color. Mica is black. Quartz is colorless. Look at the egg-shaped paperweights in **Figure 3.** The pink one is made from granite that has more feldspar than mica or quartz. That is why it is pink. The black one is made from granite that has more mica than the other minerals. The gray one is made from granite that has more quartz than the other minerals. Even though the proportions of the minerals change, this combination of minerals is always a mixture called *granite*. **Table 1** above summarizes the differences between mixtures and compounds.

Figure 3 *These paperweights are made of granite. They are different colors because the granite used in each has different ratios of minerals.*

Solutions

A **solution** is a mixture that appears to be a single substance. A solution is composed of particles of two or more substances that are distributed evenly among each other. Solutions have the same appearance and properties throughout the mixture.

The process in which particles of substances separate and spread evenly throughout a mixture is known as *dissolving*. In solutions, the **solute** is the substance that is dissolved. The **solvent** is the substance in which the solute is dissolved. A solute must be *soluble,* or able to dissolve, in the solvent. A substance that is *insoluble,* or unable to dissolve, forms a mixture that is not a solution.

Salt water is a solution. Salt is soluble in water, meaning that salt dissolves in water. So, salt is the solute, and water is the solvent. When two liquids or two gases form a solution, the substance that is present in the largest amount is the solvent.

solution a homogeneous mixture of two or more substances uniformly dispersed throughout a single phase

solute in a solution, the substance that dissolves in the solvent

solvent in a solution, the substance in which the solute dissolves

Table 2 Examples of Different States in Solutions

States	Examples
Gas in gas	dry air (oxygen in nitrogen)
Gas in liquid	soft drinks (carbon dioxide in water)
Liquid in liquid	antifreeze (alcohol in water)
Solid in liquid	salt water (salt in water)
Solid in solid	brass (zinc in copper)

Examples of Solutions

You may think that all solutions are liquids. And in fact, tap water, soft drinks, gasoline, and many cleaning supplies are liquid solutions. However, solutions may also be gases, such as air. Solutions may even be solids, such as steel. *Alloys* are solid solutions of metals or nonmetals dissolved in metals. Brass is an alloy of the metal zinc dissolved in copper. Steel is an alloy made of the nonmetal carbon and other elements dissolved in iron. **Table 2** lists more examples of solutions.

Reading Check What is an alloy?

Particles in Solutions

The particles in solutions are so small that they never settle out. They also cannot be removed by filtering. In fact, the particles are so small that they don't even scatter light. Both of the jars in **Figure 4** contain mixtures. The mixture in the jar on the left is a solution of table salt in water. The jar on the right holds a mixture—but not a solution—of gelatin in water.

CONNECTION TO Language Arts

WRITING SKILL **Alloys** Research an alloy. Find out what the alloy is made of and the amount of each substance in the alloy. Also, identify different ways that the alloy is used. Then, write a song or poem about the alloy to recite in class.

Figure 4 *Both of these jars contain mixtures. The mixture in the jar on the left, however, is a solution. The particles in solutions are so small that they don't scatter light. Therefore, you can't see the path of light through the solution.*

Figure 5 *The dilute solution (left) contains less solute than the concentrated solution (right).*

concentration the amount of a particular substance in a given quantity of a mixture, solution, or ore

solubility the ability of one substance to dissolve in another at a given temperature and pressure

Concentration of Solutions

A measure of the amount of solute dissolved in a solvent is **concentration.** Concentration can be expressed in grams of solute per milliliter of solvent (g/mL).

Concentrated or Dilute?

Solutions can be described as being concentrated or dilute. In **Figure 5,** both solutions have the same amount of solvent. However, the solution on the left contains less solute than the solution on the right. The solution on the left is dilute. The solution on the right is concentrated. Keep in mind that the terms *dilute* and *concentrated* do not tell you the amount of solute that is dissolved.

Solubility

If you add too much sugar to a glass of lemonade, not all of the sugar can dissolve. Some of it sinks to the bottom. To find the maximum amount of sugar that can dissolve, you would need to know the solubility of sugar. The **solubility** of a solute is the ability of the solute to dissolve in a solvent at a certain temperature. **Figure 6** shows how the solubility of several different solid substances changes with temperature.

Calculating Concentration What is the concentration of a solution that has 35 g of salt dissolved in 175 mL of water?

Step 1: One equation for finding concentration is the following:

$$concentration = \frac{grams\ of\ solute}{milliliters\ of\ solvent}$$

Step 2: Replace grams of solute and milliliters of solvent with the values given, and solve.

$$\frac{35\ g\ salt}{175\ mL\ water} = 0.2\ g/mL$$

Now It's Your Turn

1. What is the concentration of solution A if it has 55 g of sugar dissolved in 500 mL of water?
2. What is the concentration of solution B if it has 36 g of sugar dissolved in 144 mL of water?
3. Which solution is more concentrated?

Figure 6 **Solubility of Different Solids In Water**

The solubility of most solids increases as the temperature gets higher. So, more solute can dissolve at higher temperatures. However, some solids, such as cerium sulfate, are less soluble at higher temperatures.

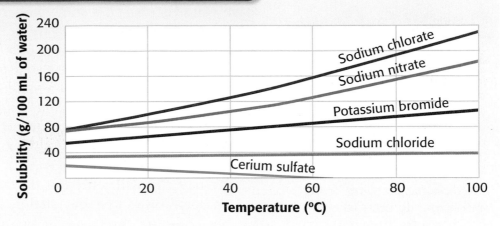

Dissolving Gases in Liquids

Most solids are more soluble in liquids at higher temperatures. But gases become less soluble in liquids as the temperature is raised. A soft drink goes flat faster when warm. The gas that is dissolved in the soft drink cannot stay dissolved when the temperature increases. So, the gas escapes, and the soft drink becomes "flat."

✓ Reading Check How does the solubility of gases change with temperature?

Dissolving Solids Faster in Liquids

Several things affect how fast a solid will dissolve. Look at **Figure 7** to see three ways to make a solute dissolve faster. You can see why you will enjoy a glass of lemonade sooner if you stir granulated sugar into the lemonade before adding ice!

Figure 7 **How to Dissolve Solids Faster**

Mixing by stirring or shaking causes the solute particles to separate from one another and spread out more quickly among the solvent particles.

Heating causes particles to move more quickly. The solvent particles can separate the solute particles and spread them out more quickly.

Crushing the solute increases the amount of contact it has with the solvent. The particles of the crushed solute mix with the solvent more quickly.

Suspensions

Many household items, such as paints, salad dressings, and medicines, are suspensions. With an adult, find several items that have directions that tell you to shake the bottle before use. Discuss what problems could arise if you do not shake the container before use.

suspension a mixture in which particles of a material are more or less evenly dispersed throughout a liquid or gas

colloid a mixture consisting of tiny particles that are intermediate in size between those in solutions and those in suspensions and that are suspended in a liquid, solid, or gas

Suspensions

Have you ever shaken a snow globe? If so, you have seen the solid snow particles mix with the water, as shown in **Figure 8.** When you stop shaking the globe, the snow settles to the bottom. This mixture is called a suspension. A **suspension** is a mixture in which particles of a material are dispersed throughout a liquid or gas but are large enough that they settle out.

The particles in a suspension are large enough to scatter or block light. The particles are also too large to stay mixed without being stirred or shaken. If a suspension is allowed to sit, the particles will settle out, as they do in a snow globe.

A suspension can be separated by passing it through a filter. So, the liquid or gas passes through the filter, but the solid particles are large enough to be trapped by the filter.

✓ Reading Check How can the particles of a suspension be separated?

Colloids

Some mixtures have properties between those of solutions and suspensions. These mixtures are known as colloids (KAHL OYDZ). A **colloid** is a mixture in which the particles are dispersed throughout but are not heavy enough to settle out. The particles in a colloid are relatively small and are fairly well mixed. You might be surprised at the number of colloids you see each day. Milk, mayonnaise, and stick deodorant—even the gelatin and whipped cream in **Figure 8**—are colloids.

The particles in a colloid are much smaller than the particles in a suspension. However, the particles are large enough to scatter light. A colloid cannot be separated by filtration. The particles are small enough to pass through a filter.

Figure 8 **Properties of Suspensions and Colloids**

Suspension This snow globe contains solid particles that will mix with the clear liquid when you shake it up. But the particles will soon fall to the bottom when the globe is at rest.

Colloid This dessert includes two tasty examples of colloids—fruity gelatin and whipped cream.

Summary

- A mixture is a combination of two or more substances, each of which keeps its own characteristics.
- Mixtures can be separated by physical means, such as filtration and evaporation.
- A solution is a mixture that appears to be a single substance but is composed of a solute dissolved in a solvent.
- Concentration is a measure of the amount of solute dissolved in a solvent.

- The solubility of a solute is the ability of the solute to dissolve in a solvent at a certain temperature.
- Suspensions are mixtures that contain particles large enough to settle out or be filtered and to block or scatter light.
- Colloids are mixtures that contain particles that are too small to settle out or be filtered but are large enough to scatter light.

Using Key Terms

The statements below are false. For each statement, replace the underlined term to make a true statement.

1. The <u>solvent</u> is the substance that is dissolved.

2. A <u>suspension</u> is composed of substances that are spread evenly among each other.

3. A measure of the amount of solute dissolved in a solvent is <u>solubility</u>.

4. A <u>colloid</u> contains particles that will settle out of the mixture if left sitting.

Understanding Key Ideas

5. A mixture
   a. has substances in it that are chemically combined.
   b. can always be separated using filtration.
   c. contains substances that are not mixed in a definite ratio.
   d. All of the above

6. List three ways to dissolve a solid faster.

Critical Thinking

7. **Making Comparisons** How do solutions, suspensions, and colloids differ?

8. **Applying Concepts** Suggest a procedure to separate iron filings from sawdust. Explain why this procedure works.

9. **Analyzing Ideas** Identify the solute and solvent in a solution made of 15 mL of oxygen and 5 mL of helium.

Interpreting Graphics

Use the graph below to answer the questions that follow.

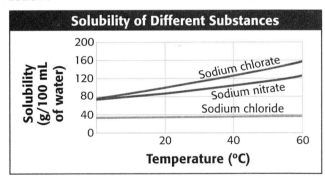

Solubility of Different Substances

10. At what temperature is 120 g of sodium nitrate soluble in 100 mL of water?

11. At 60°C, how much more sodium chlorate than sodium chloride will dissolve in 100 mL of water?

Skills Practice Lab

Flame Tests

Fireworks produce fantastic combinations of color when they are ignited. The different colors are the results of burning different compounds. Imagine that you are the head chemist for a fireworks company. The label has fallen off one box, and you must identify the unknown compound inside so that the fireworks may be used in the correct fireworks display. To identify the compound, you will use your knowledge that every compound has a unique set of properties.

Ask a Question

1 How can you identify an unknown compound by heating it in a flame?

Form a Hypothesis

2 Write a hypothesis that is a possible answer to the question above. Explain your reasoning.

Test the Hypothesis

3 Arrange the test tubes in the test-tube rack. Use masking tape to label each tube with one of the following names: calcium chloride, potassium chloride, sodium chloride, and unknown.

4 Copy the table below. Then, ask your teacher for your portions of the solutions. **Caution:** Be very careful in handling all chemicals. Tell your teacher immediately if you spill a chemical.

Test Results	
Compound	**Color of flame**
Calcium chloride	
Potassium chloride	DO NOT WRITE IN BOOK
Sodium chloride	
Unknown	

OBJECTIVES

Observe flame colors emitted by various compounds.

Determine the composition of an unknown compound.

MATERIALS

- Bunsen burner
- chloride test solutions (4)
- hydrochloric acid, dilute, in a small beaker
- spark igniter
- tape, masking
- test tubes, small (4)
- test-tube rack
- water, distilled, in a small beaker
- wire and holder

SAFETY

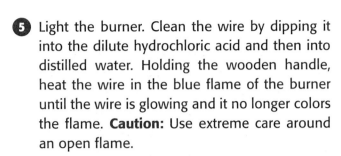

5 Light the burner. Clean the wire by dipping it into the dilute hydrochloric acid and then into distilled water. Holding the wooden handle, heat the wire in the blue flame of the burner until the wire is glowing and it no longer colors the flame. **Caution:** Use extreme care around an open flame.

6 Dip the clean wire into the first test solution. Hold the wire at the tip of the inner cone of the burner flame. Record in the table the color given to the flame.

7 Clean the wire by repeating step 5. Then, repeat steps 5 and 6 for the other solutions.

8 Follow your teacher's instructions for cleanup and disposal.

Analyze the Results

1 **Identifying Patterns** Is the flame color a test for the metal or for the chloride in each compound? Explain your answer.

2 **Analyzing Data** What is the identity of your unknown solution? How do you know?

Draw Conclusions

3 **Evaluating Methods** Why is it necessary to carefully clean the wire before testing each solution?

4 **Making Predictions** Would you expect the compound sodium fluoride to produce the same color as sodium chloride in a flame test? Why or why not?

5 **Interpreting Information** Each of the compounds you tested is made from chlorine, which is a poisonous gas at room temperature. Why is it safe to use these compounds without a gas mask?

Chapter Review

USING KEY TERMS

Complete each of the following sentences by choosing the correct term from the word bank.

compound   element
suspension   solubility
solution   metal
nonmetal   solute

1 A(n) ___ has a definite ratio of components.

2 The ability of one substance to dissolve in another substance is the ___ of the solute.

3 A(n) ___ can be separated by filtration.

4 A(n) ___ is a pure substance that cannot be broken down into simpler substances by chemical means.

5 A(n) ___ is an element that is brittle and dull.

6 The ___ is the substance that dissolves to form a solution.

UNDERSTANDING KEY IDEAS

Multiple Choice

7 Which of the following increases the solubility of a gas in a liquid?

a. increasing the temperature of the liquid

b. increasing the amount of gas in the liquid

c. decreasing the temperature of the liquid

d. decreasing the amount of liquid

8 Which of the following best describes chicken noodle soup?

a. element   **c.** compound

b. mixture   **d.** solution

9 Which of the following statements describes elements?

a. All of the particles in the same element are different.

b. Elements can be broken down into simpler substances.

c. Elements have unique sets of properties.

d. Elements cannot be joined together in chemical reactions.

10 A solution that contains a large amount of solute is best described as

a. insoluble.   **c.** dilute.

b. concentrated.   **d.** weak.

11 Which of the following substances can be separated into simpler substances only by chemical means?

a. sodium   **c.** water

b. salt water   **d.** gold

12 Which of the following would not increase the rate at which a solid dissolves?

a. decreasing the temperature

b. crushing the solid

c. stirring

d. increasing the temperature

13 In which classification of matter are components chemically combined?

   a. a solution   **c.** a compound

   b. a colloid   **d.** a suspension

14 An element that conducts thermal energy well and is easily shaped is a

   a. metal.

   b. metalloid.

   c. nonmetal.

   d. None of the above

Short Answer

15 What is the difference between an element and a compound?

16 When nail polish is dissolved in acetone, which substance is the solute, and which is the solvent?

Math Skills

17 What is the concentration of a solution prepared by mixing 50 g of salt with 200 mL of water?

18 How many grams of sugar must be dissolved in 150 mL of water to make a solution that has a concentration of 0.6 g/mL?

CRITICAL THINKING

19 **Concept Mapping** Use the following terms to create a concept map: *matter, element, compound, mixture, solution, suspension,* and *colloid*.

20 **Forming Hypotheses** To keep the "fizz" in carbonated beverages after they have been opened, should you store them in a refrigerator or in a cabinet? Explain.

21 **Making Inferences** A light green powder is heated in a test tube. A gas is given off, and the solid becomes black. In which classification of matter does the green powder belong? Explain your reasoning.

22 **Predicting Consequences** Why is it desirable to know the exact concentration of solutions rather than whether they are concentrated or dilute?

23 **Applying Concepts** Describe a procedure to separate a mixture of salt, finely ground pepper, and pebbles.

INTERPRETING GRAPHICS

Dr. Sol Vent did an experiment to find the solubility of a compound. The data below were collected using 100 mL of water. Use the table below to answer the questions that follow.

Temperature (°C)	10	25	40	60	95
Dissolved solute (g)	150	70	34	25	15

24 Use a computer or graph paper to construct a graph of Dr. Vent's results. Examine the graph. To increase the solubility, would you increase or decrease the temperature? Explain.

25 If 200 mL of water were used instead of 100 mL, how many grams of the compound would dissolve at 40°C?

26 Based on the solubility of this compound, is this compound a solid, liquid, or gas? Explain your answer.

Standardized Test Preparation

Read each of the passages below. Then, answer the questions that follow each passage.

Passage 1 In 1912, the *Titanic* was the largest ship ever to set sail. This majestic ship was considered to be unsinkable. Yet, on April 15, 1912, the *Titanic* hit a large iceberg. The resulting damage caused the *Titanic* to sink, killing 1,500 of its passengers and crew.

How could an iceberg destroy the 2.5 cm thick steel plates that made up the *Titanic*'s hull? Analysis of a recovered piece of steel showed that the steel contained large amounts of sulfur. Sulfur is a normal component of steel. However, the recovered piece has much more sulfur than today's steel does. The excess sulfur may have made the steel <u>brittle</u>, much like glass. Scientists suspect that this brittle steel may have cracked on impact with the iceberg, allowing water to enter the hull.

1. In this passage, what does the word *brittle* mean?

   A likely to break or crack

   B very strong

   C clear and easily seen through

   D lightweight

2. What is the main idea of the second paragraph of this passage?

   F The *Titanic*'s hull was 2.5 cm thick.

   G The steel in the *Titanic*'s hull may have been brittle.

   H The large amount of sulfur in the *Titanic*'s hull may be responsible for the hull's cracking.

   I Scientists were able to recover a piece of steel from the *Titanic*'s hull.

3. What was the *Titanic* thought to be in 1912?

   A the fastest ship afloat

   B the smallest ship to set sail

   C a ship not capable of being sunk

   D the most luxurious ship to set sail

Passage 2 Perfume making is an ancient art. It was practiced by the ancient Egyptians, who rubbed their bodies with a substance made by soaking fragrant woods and resins in water and oil. Ancient Israelites also practiced the art of perfume making. This art was also known to the early Chinese, Arabs, Greeks, and Romans.

Over time, perfume making has developed into a fine art. A good perfume may contain more than 100 ingredients. The most familiar ingredients come from fragrant plants, such as sandalwood or roses. These plants get their pleasant odor from essential oils, which are stored in tiny, baglike parts called *sacs*. The parts of plants that are used for perfumes include the flowers, roots, and leaves. Other perfume ingredients come from animals and from human-made chemicals.

1. How did ancient Egyptians make perfume?

   A by using 100 different ingredients

   B by soaking woods and resins in water and oil

   C by using plants or flowers

   D by making tiny, baglike parts called sacs

2. What is the main idea of the second paragraph?

   F Perfume making hasn't changed since ancient Egypt.

   G The ancient art of perfume making has been replaced by simple science.

   H Perfume making is a complex procedure involving many ingredients.

   I Natural ingredients are no longer used in perfume.

3. How are good perfumes made?

   A from plant oils only

   B by combining one or two ingredients

   C according to early Chinese formulas

   D by blending as many as 100 ingredients

The graph below was constructed from data collected during a laboratory investigation. Use the graph below to answer the questions that follow.

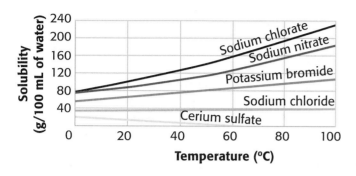

1. Which of the following values is the amount of sodium nitrate that can dissolve in 100 mL of water at 40°C?

   A 0 g

   B 40 g

   C 80 g

   D 100 g

2. How many grams of sodium chloride can dissolve in 100 mL of water at 60°C?

   F 40 g

   G 80 g

   H 125 g

   I 160 g

3. At what temperature will 80 g of potassium bromide completely dissolve in 100 mL of water?

   A approximately 20°C

   B approximately 42°C

   C approximately 88°C

   D approximately 100°C

4. At 20°C, which solid is the most soluble?

   F sodium chloride

   G sodium chlorate

   H potassium bromide

   I sodium nitrate

Read each question below, and choose the best answer.

Use the rectangle below to answer questions 1 and 2.

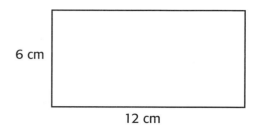

1. What is the perimeter of the rectangle shown above?

   A 12 cm

   B 18 cm

   C 36 cm

   D 72 cm

2. If the length of all the sides of the rectangle shown above were doubled, what would be the area of the larger rectangle?

   F 36 cm²

   G 72 cm²

   H 144 cm²

   I 288 cm²

3. One way to calculate the concentration of a solution is to divide the grams of solute by the milliliters of solvent. What is the concentration of a solution that is made by dissolving 65 g of sugar (the solute) in 500 mL of water (the solvent)?

   A 0.13 g·mL

   B 0.13 g/mL

   C 7.7 g·mL

   D 7.7 g/mL

4. If 16/n = 1/2, what is the value of *n*?

   F 2

   G 8

   H 16

   I 32

Science in Action

Science, Technology, and Society

Dry Cleaning: How Stains Are Dissolved

Sometimes, just water and detergent won't remove stains. For example, have you gotten ink on your favorite sweater? Or have you spilled something greasy on your shirt? In that case, your clothes will probably have to be dry-cleaned. In spite of its name, dry cleaning does involve liquids. First, the kind of stain on your clothing must be determined. If the stain will dissolve in water, a stain remover for that particular stain is applied. Then, the stain is removed with a steam gun. But some stains, such as grease or oil, won't dissolve in water. This kind of stain is treated with a liquid solvent. The clothing is then cleaned in a dry-cleaning machine.

Language Arts ACTiViTy

WRITING SKILL Imagine that you are a stained article of clothing. Write a five-paragraph short story describing how you became stained and how the stain was removed by the dry-cleaning process. You may have to research the dry-cleaning process before writing your story.

Science Fiction

"The Strange Case of Dr. Jekyll and Mr. Hyde" by Robert Louis Stevenson

Although Dr. Henry Jekyll was wild as a young man, he has become a respected doctor and scientist. Dr. Jekyll wants to understand the nature of human identity. His theory is that if he can separate his personality into "good" and "evil" parts, he can get rid of his evil side. Then, he can lead a happy, useful life.

Into Dr. Jekyll's life comes the mysterious Mr. Hyde, a man of action and anger. He sparks fear in the hearts of people he meets. Who is he? And what does he have to do with the deaths of two people? To find out more, read Stevenson's "The Strange Case of Dr. Jekyll and Mr. Hyde" in the *Holt Anthology of Science Fiction*.

Social Studies ACTiViTy

"The Strange Case of Dr. Jekyll and Mr. Hyde" was published in 1886. The story takes place in London, England. What was London like in the 1870s and 1880s? Use the library or the Internet to find information about London and its people at that time. Make a chart that compares London in the 1870s with your hometown today.

Aundra Nix

Metallurgist Aundra Nix is a chief metallurgist for a copper mine in Sahuarita, Arizona, where she supervises laboratories and other engineers. "To be able to look at rock in the ground and follow it through a process of drilling, blasting, hauling, crushing, grinding, and finally mineral separation—where you can hold a mineral that is one-third copper in your hand—is exciting."

Although she is a supervisor, Nix enjoys the flexible nature of her job. "My work environment includes office and computer work, plant work, and outdoor work. In this field you can 'get your hands into it,' which I always prefer," says Nix. "I did not want a career where it may be years before you see the results of your work." Aundra Nix enjoyed math and science, "so engineering seemed to be a natural area to study," she says. Nix's advice to students planning their own career is to learn all they can in science and technology, because that is the future.

Math ACTIVITY

A large copper-mining company employed about 2,300 people at three locations in New Mexico. Because of an increase in demand for copper, 570 of these workers were hired over a period of a year. Of the 570 new workers, 115 were hired within a three-week period. What percentage of the total work force do the newly hired employees represent? Of the new workers who were hired, what percentage was hired during the three-week hiring period?

To learn more about these Science in Action topics, visit **go.hrw.com** and type in the keyword **HP5MIXF.**

Current Science

Check out Current Science® articles related to this chapter by visiting go.hrw.com. Just type in the keyword **HP5CS04.**

Introduction to Atoms

4

The Big Idea

Atoms are composed of small particles that determine the properties of the atom.

About the PHOTO

You have probably made bubbles with a plastic wand and a soapy liquid. Some scientists make bubbles by using a bubble chamber. A bubble chamber is filled with a pressurized liquid that forms bubbles when a charged particle moves through it. This photo shows the tracks made by charged particles moving through a bubble chamber. Bubble chambers help scientists learn about particles called *atoms*, which make up all objects.

PRE-READING ACTIVITY

Graphic Organizer

Chain-of-Events Chart Before you read the chapter, create the graphic organizer entitled "Chain-of-Events Chart" described in the **Study Skills** section of the Appendix. As you read the chapter, fill in the chart with details about each step in the historical development of ideas about atoms.

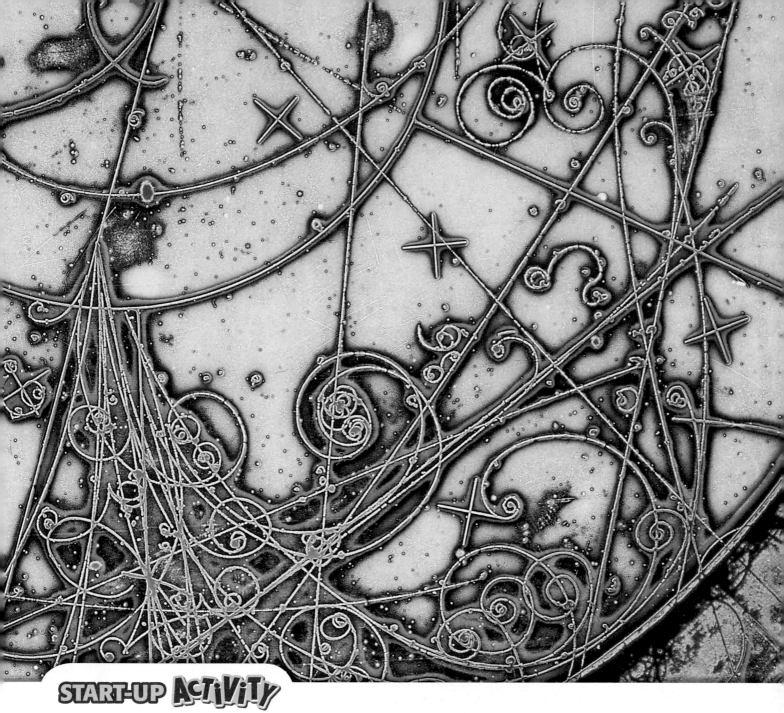

START-UP ACTIVITY

Where Is It?

Scientists have been able to gather information about atoms without actually seeing them. In this activity, you will do something similar: you will form an idea about the location and size of a hidden object by rolling marbles at it.

Procedure

1. Place a **rectangular piece of cardboard** on **four books or blocks** so that each corner of the cardboard rests on a book or block.

2. Your teacher will place an **unknown object** under the cardboard. Be sure that you cannot see the object.

3. Place a **large piece of paper** on top of the cardboard.

4. Carefully roll a **marble** under the cardboard. Record on the paper the position where the marble enters and exits. Also, record the direction it travels.

5. Keep rolling the marble from different directions to collect data about the shape and location of the object. Write down all of your observations.

Analysis

1. Form a conclusion about the object's shape, size, and location. Record your conclusion.

2. Lift the cardboard, and look at the object. Compare your conclusions with the object's actual size, shape, and location.

Development of the Atomic Theory

Have you ever watched a mystery movie and thought you knew who the criminal was? Have you ever changed your mind because of a new fact or clue?

The same thing happens in science! Sometimes an idea or model must be changed as new information is gathered. In this section, you will see how our ideas about atoms have changed over time. Your first stop is ancient Greece.

The Beginning of Atomic Theory

Imagine that you cut something in half. Then, you cut each half in half again, and so on. Could you keep cutting the pieces in half forever? Around 440 BCE, a Greek philosopher named Democritus (di MAHK ruh tuhs) thought that you would eventually end up with a particle that could not be cut. He called this particle an atom. The word *atom* is from the Greek word *atomos,* meaning "not able to be divided." Democritus said that all atoms are small, hard particles. He thought that atoms were made of a single material formed into different shapes and sizes.

What You Will Learn

- Describe some of the experiments that led to the current atomic theory.
- Compare the different models of the atom.
- Explain how the atomic theory has changed as scientists have discovered new information about the atom.

Vocabulary

atom
electron
nucleus
electron cloud

READING STRATEGY

Reading Organizer As you read this section, create an outline of the section. Use the headings from the section in your outline.

From Aristotle to Modern Science

Aristotle (AR is TAHT'l), another Greek philosopher, disagreed with Democritus's ideas. He believed that you would never end up with a particle that could not be cut. He had such a strong influence on people's ideas that for a long time, most people thought he was right.

Democritus was right, though: Matter is made of particles, which we call atoms. An **atom** is the smallest particle into which an element can be divided and still be the same substance. **Figure 1** shows a picture of aluminum atoms taken with a scanning tunneling electron microscope (STM). Long before actually being able to scan atoms, scientists had ideas about them.

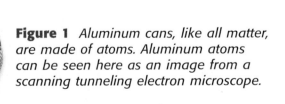

Figure 1 *Aluminum cans, like all matter, are made of atoms. Aluminum atoms can be seen here as an image from a scanning tunneling electron microscope.*

Dalton's Atomic Theory Based on Experiments

By the late 1700s, scientists had learned that elements combine in certain proportions based on mass to form compounds. For example, hydrogen and oxygen always combine in the same proportion to form water. John Dalton, a British chemist and schoolteacher, wanted to know why. He experimented with different substances. His results suggested that elements combine in certain proportions because they are made of single atoms. Dalton, shown in **Figure 2,** published his atomic theory in 1803. His theory stated the following ideas:

atom the smallest unit of an element that maintains the properties of that element

- All substances are made of atoms. Atoms are small particles that cannot be created, divided, or destroyed.

- Atoms of the same element are exactly alike, and atoms of different elements are different.

- Atoms join with other atoms to make new substances.

✓ Reading Check Why did Dalton think that elements are made of single atoms? (*See the Appendix for answers to Reading Checks.*)

Not Quite Correct

Toward the end of the 1800s, scientists agreed that Dalton's theory explained much of what they saw. However, new information was found that did not fit some of Dalton's ideas. The atomic theory was then changed to describe the atom more correctly. As you read on, you will learn how Dalton's theory has changed, step by step, into the modern atomic theory.

Figure 2 *John Dalton developed his atomic theory from observations gathered from many experiments.*

Figure 3 **Thomson's Cathode-Ray Tube Experiment**

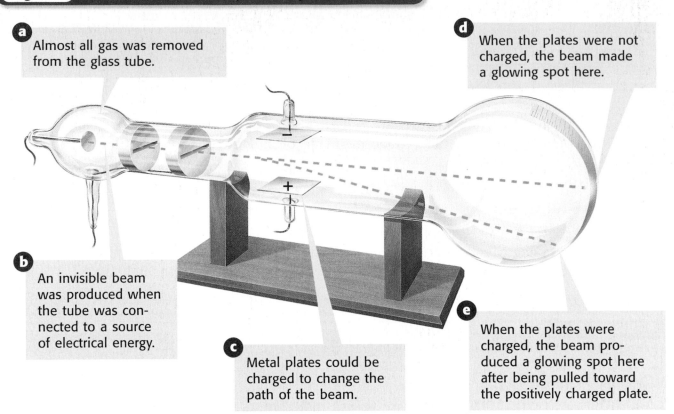

a Almost all gas was removed from the glass tube.

d When the plates were not charged, the beam made a glowing spot here.

b An invisible beam was produced when the tube was connected to a source of electrical energy.

c Metal plates could be charged to change the path of the beam.

e When the plates were charged, the beam produced a glowing spot here after being pulled toward the positively charged plate.

Thomson's Discovery of Electrons

In 1897, a British scientist named J. J. Thomson showed that there was a mistake in Dalton's theory. Thomson discovered that there are small particles *inside* the atom. This means that atoms can be divided into even smaller parts.

Thomson experimented with a cathode-ray tube like the one shown in **Figure 3.** He discovered that a positively charged plate (marked with a plus sign in the drawing) attracted the beam. Thomson concluded that the beam was made of particles that have negative electric charges. He also concluded that these negatively charged particles are present in every kind of atom. The negatively charged particles that Thomson discovered are now called **electrons.**

electron a subatomic particle that has a negative charge

Like Plums in a Pudding

After learning that atoms contain electrons, Thomson proposed a new model of the atom. This model is shown in **Figure 4.** It is sometimes called the *plum-pudding model,* after a dessert that was popular in Thomson's day. Thomson thought that electrons were mixed throughout an atom, like plums in a pudding. Today, you might call Thomson's model the *chocolate chip ice-cream model.*

Figure 4 *Thomson proposed that electrons were located throughout an atom like plums in a pudding, as shown in this model.*

Rutherford's Atomic "Shooting Gallery"

In 1909, a former student of Thomson's named Ernest Rutherford decided to test Thomson's theory. He designed an experiment to study the parts of the atom. He aimed a beam of small, positively charged particles at a thin sheet of gold foil. **Figure 5** shows Rutherford's experiment. Rutherford put a special coating behind the foil. The coating glowed when hit by the positively charged particles. Rutherford could then see where the particles went after hitting the gold.

✓ **Reading Check** How could Rutherford tell where the positively charged particles went after hitting the gold foil?

Surprising Results

Rutherford started with Thomson's idea that atoms are soft "blobs" of matter. He expected the particles to pass right through the gold in a straight line. Most of the particles did just that. But to Rutherford's great surprise, some of the particles were deflected (turned to one side). Some even bounced straight back. Rutherford reportedly said,

"It was quite the most incredible event that has ever happened to me in my life. It was almost as if you fired a fifteen-inch shell into a piece of tissue paper and it came back and hit you."

CONNECTION TO Language Arts

WRITING SKILL **Solving Mysteries** Scientists who made discoveries about the atom had to do so by gathering clues and drawing conclusions from experiments. Read a short mystery story, and write a one-page paper in which you discuss the methods that were used to solve the mystery in the story. Compare these methods with those used by scientists finding out about what atoms are like.

Figure 5 Rutherford's Gold-Foil Experiment

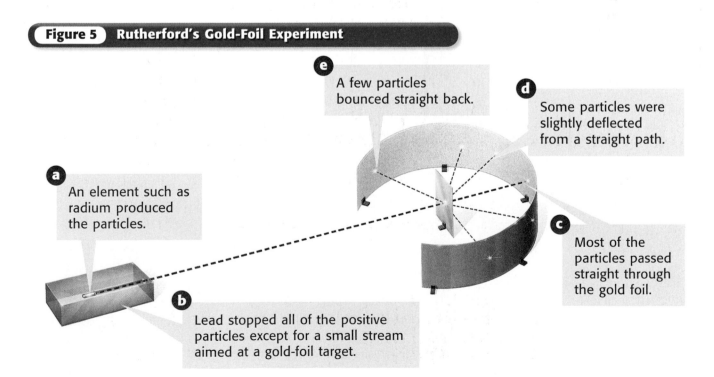

e A few particles bounced straight back.

d Some particles were slightly deflected from a straight path.

a An element such as radium produced the particles.

c Most of the particles passed straight through the gold foil.

b Lead stopped all of the positive particles except for a small stream aimed at a gold-foil target.

nucleus in physical science, an atom's central region, which is made up of protons and neutrons

electron cloud a region around the nucleus of an atom where electrons are likely to be found

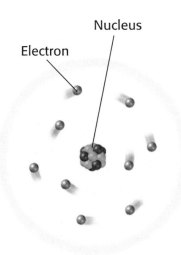

Electron
Nucleus

Figure 6 *Rutherford's model of the atom had electrons surrounding the nucleus at a distance. (This model does not show the true scale of sizes and distances.)*

Where Are the Electrons?

The plum-pudding model of the atom did not explain what Rutherford saw. Most of the tiny particles went straight through the gold foil, with a small number being deflected. He realized that in order to explain this, atoms must be considered mostly empty space, with a tiny part made of highly dense matter.

Far from the Nucleus

In 1911, Rutherford revised the atomic theory. He made a new model of the atom, as shown in **Figure 6.** Rutherford proposed that in the center of the atom is a tiny, extremely dense, positively charged part called the **nucleus** (NOO klee uhs). Because like charges repel, Rutherford reasoned that positively charged particles that passed close by the nucleus were pushed away by the positive charges in the nucleus. A particle that headed straight for a nucleus would be pushed almost straight back in the direction from which it came. From his results, Rutherford calculated that the diameter of the nucleus was 100,000 times smaller than the diameter of the gold atom. To get an idea of this kind of difference in size, look at **Figure 7.**

✓ **Reading Check** How did Rutherford change Thomson's model of the atom?

Bohr's Electron Levels

In 1913, Niels Bohr, a Danish scientist who worked with Rutherford, studied the way that atoms react to light. Bohr's results led him to propose that electrons move around the nucleus in certain paths, or energy levels. In Bohr's model, there are no paths between the levels. But electrons can jump from a path in one level to a path in another level. Think of the levels as rungs on a ladder. You can stand on the rungs of a ladder but not *between* the rungs. Bohr's model was a valuable tool in predicting some atomic behavior, but the atomic theory still had room for improvement.

Figure 7 *The diameter of this pinhead is 100,000 times smaller than the diameter of the stadium. The pinhead represents the size of a nucleus, and the stadium represents the size of an atom.*

The Modern Atomic Theory

Many 20th-century scientists added to our current understanding of the atom. An Austrian physicist named Erwin Schrödinger (SHROH ding uhr) and a German physicist named Werner Heisenberg (HIE zuhn berkh) did especially important work. They further explained the nature of electrons in the atom. For example, electrons do not travel in definite paths as Bohr suggested. In fact, the exact path of an electron cannot be predicted. According to the current theory, there are regions inside the atom where electrons are *likely* to be found. These regions are called **electron clouds**. The electron-cloud model of the atom is shown in **Figure 8**.

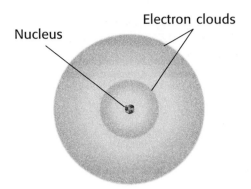

Nucleus

Electron clouds

Figure 8 *In the current model of the atom, electrons surround the nucleus in electron clouds.*

SECTION
Review

Summary

- Democritus thought that matter is composed of atoms.
- Dalton based his theory on observations of how elements combine.
- Thomson discovered electrons in atoms.
- Rutherford discovered that atoms are mostly empty space with a dense, positive nucleus.
- Bohr proposed that electrons are located in levels at certain distances from the nucleus.
- The electron-cloud model represents the current atomic theory.

Using Key Terms

1. In your own words, write a definition for the term *atom*.

The statements below are false. For each statement, replace the underlined term to make a true statement.

2. A <u>nucleus</u> is a particle with a negative electric charge.

3. The <u>electron</u> is where most of an atom's mass is located.

Understanding Key Ideas

4. Which of the following scientists discovered that atoms contain electrons?
   a. Dalton
   b. Thomson
   c. Rutherford
   d. Bohr

5. What did Dalton do in developing his theory that Democritus did not do?

6. What discovery demonstrated that atoms are mostly empty space?

7. What refinements did Bohr make to Rutherford's proposed atomic theory?

Critical Thinking

8. **Making Comparisons** Compare the location of electrons in Bohr's theory with the location of electrons in the current atomic theory.

9. **Analyzing Methods** How does the design of Rutherford's experiment show what he was trying to find out?

Interpreting Graphics

10. What about the atomic model shown below was shown to be incorrect?

SciLINKS

NSTA
Developed and maintained by the
National Science Teachers Association

For a variety of links related to this chapter, go to www.scilinks.org
Topic: Development of the Atomic Theory; Current Atomic Theory
SciLinks code: HSM0399; HSM0371

The Atom

Even though atoms are very small, they are made up of even smaller things. You can learn a lot about the parts that make up an atom and what holds an atom together.

In this section, you'll learn about how atoms are alike and how they are different. But first you'll find out just how small an atom really is.

How Small Is an Atom?

Think about a penny. A penny contains about 2×10^{22} atoms (which can be written as 20,000,000,000,000,000,000,000 atoms) of copper and zinc. That's 20 thousand billion billion atoms—over 3,000,000,000,000 times more atoms than there are people on Earth! If there are that many atoms in a penny, each atom must be very small.

Scientists know that aluminum is made of average-sized atoms. An aluminum atom has a diameter of about 0.00000003 cm. That's three one-hundred-millionths of a centimeter. Take a look at **Figure 1.** Even things that are very thin, such as aluminum foil, are made up of very large numbers of atoms.

Figure 1 *This aluminum foil might seem thin to you. But it is about 50,000 atoms thick!*

Figure 2 Parts of an Atom

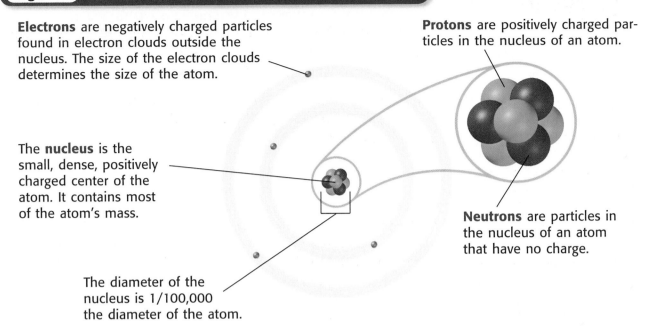

Electrons are negatively charged particles found in electron clouds outside the nucleus. The size of the electron clouds determines the size of the atom.

Protons are positively charged particles in the nucleus of an atom.

The **nucleus** is the small, dense, positively charged center of the atom. It contains most of the atom's mass.

Neutrons are particles in the nucleus of an atom that have no charge.

The diameter of the nucleus is 1/100,000 the diameter of the atom.

What Is an Atom Made Of?

As tiny as an atom is, it is made up of even smaller particles. These particles are protons, neutrons, and electrons, shown in the model in **Figure 2.** (The particles in the pictures are not shown in their correct proportions. If they were, the electrons would be too small to see.)

The Nucleus

Protons are positively charged particles in the nucleus. The mass of a proton is about 1.7×10^{-24} g. This number can also be written as 0.0000000000000000000000017 g. Because the masses of particles in atoms are so small, scientists made a new unit for them. The SI unit used to express the masses of particles in atoms is the **atomic mass unit** (amu). Each proton has a mass of about 1 amu.

Neutrons are the particles of the nucleus that have no electrical charge. Neutrons are a little more massive than protons are. But the difference in mass is so small that the mass of a neutron can be thought of as 1 amu.

Protons and neutrons are the most massive particles in an atom. But the volume of the nucleus is very small. So, the nucleus is very dense. If it were possible to have a nucleus the volume of a grape, that nucleus would have a mass greater than 9 million metric tons!

✓ Reading Check Name the two kinds of particles that can be found in the nucleus. (*See the Appendix for answers to Reading Checks.*)

proton a subatomic particle that has a positive charge and that is found in the nucleus of an atom

atomic mass unit a unit of mass that describes the mass of an atom or molecule

neutron a subatomic particle that has no charge and that is found in the nucleus of an atom

Hydrogen Hydrogen is the most abundant element in the universe. It is the fuel for the sun and other stars. It is currently believed that there are roughly 2,000 times more hydrogen atoms than oxygen atoms and 10,000 times more hydrogen atoms than carbon atoms.

Make a model of a hydrogen atom using materials of your choice to represent a hydrogen atom's proton and electron. Present the model to the class, and explain in what ways your model resembles a hydrogen atom.

ACTIVITY

Proton

Neutron

Electron

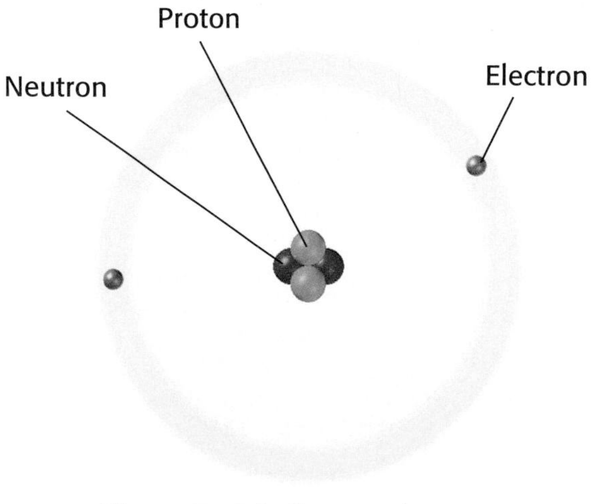

Figure 3 *A helium nucleus must have neutrons in it to keep the protons from moving apart.*

Outside the Nucleus

Electrons are the negatively charged particles in atoms. Electrons are found around the nucleus within electron clouds. Compared with protons and neutrons, electrons are very small in mass. It takes more than 1,800 electrons to equal the mass of 1 proton. The mass of an electron is so small that it is usually thought of as almost zero.

The charges of protons and electrons are opposite but equal, so their charges cancel out. Because an atom has no overall charge, it is neutral. What happens if the numbers of electrons and protons are not equal? The atom becomes a charged particle called an *ion* (IE ahn). An atom that loses one or more electrons becomes a positively-charged ion. An atom that gains one or more electrons becomes a negatively-charged ion.

✓ **Reading Check** How does an atom become a positively-charged ion?

How Do Atoms of Different Elements Differ?

There are more than 110 different elements. The atoms of each of these elements are different from the atoms of all other elements. What makes atoms different from each other? To find out, imagine that you could build an atom by putting together protons, neutrons, and electrons.

Starting Simply

It's easiest to start with the simplest atom. Protons and electrons are found in all atoms. The simplest atom is made of just one of each. It's so simple it doesn't even have a neutron. To "build" this atom, put just one proton in the center of the atom for the nucleus. Then, put one electron in the electron cloud. Congratulations! You have just made a hydrogen atom.

Now for Some Neutrons

Now, build an atom that has two protons. Both of the protons are positively charged, so they repel one another. You cannot form a nucleus with them unless you add some neutrons. For this atom, two neutrons will do. To have a neutral charge, your new atom will also need two electrons outside the nucleus. What you have is an atom of the element helium. A model of this atom is shown in **Figure 3**.

Building Bigger Atoms

You could build a carbon atom using 6 protons, 6 neutrons, and 6 electrons. You could build an oxygen atom using 8 protons, 9 neutrons, and 8 electrons. You could even build a gold atom with 79 protons, 118 neutrons, and 79 electrons! As you can see, an atom does not have to have equal numbers of protons and neutrons.

Protons and Atomic Number

How can you tell which elements these atoms represent? The key is the number of protons. The number of protons in the nucleus of an atom is the **atomic number** of that atom. All atoms of an element have the same atomic number. Every hydrogen atom has only one proton in its nucleus, so hydrogen has an atomic number of 1. Every carbon atom has six protons in its nucleus. So, carbon has an atomic number of 6.

Isotopes

An atom that has one proton, one electron, and one neutron is shown in **Figure 4.** The atomic number of this new atom is 1, so the atom is hydrogen. However, this hydrogen atom's nucleus has two particles. Therefore, this atom has a greater mass than the hydrogen atom you made.

The new atom is another isotope (IE suh TOHP) of hydrogen. **Isotopes** are atoms that have the same number of protons but have different numbers of neutrons. Atoms that are isotopes of each other are always the same element, because isotopes always have the same number of protons. They have different numbers of neutrons, however, which gives them different masses.

INTERNET ACTIVITY

For another activity related to this chapter, go to **go.hrw.com** and type in the keyword **HP5ATSW.**

atomic number the number of protons in the nucleus of an atom; the atomic number is the same for all atoms of an element

isotope an atom that has the same number of protons (or the same atomic number) as other atoms of the same element do but that has a different number of neutrons (and thus a different atomic mass)

Figure 4 **Isotopes of Hydrogen**

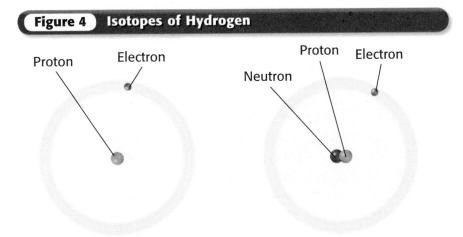

This isotope is a hydrogen atom that has one proton in its nucleus.

This isotope is a hydrogen atom that has one proton and one neutron in its nucleus.

mass number the sum of the numbers of protons and neutrons in the nucleus of an atom

Properties of Isotopes

Each element has a limited number of isotopes that are found in nature. Some isotopes of an element have special properties because they are unstable. An unstable atom is an atom with a nucleus that will change over time. This type of isotope is *radioactive*. Radioactive atoms spontaneously fall apart after a certain amount of time. As they do, they give off smaller particles, as well as energy.

However, isotopes of an element share most of the same chemical and physical properties. For example, the most common oxygen isotope has 8 neutrons in the nucleus. Other isotopes of oxygen have 9 or 10 neutrons. All three isotopes are colorless, odorless gases at room temperature. Each isotope has the chemical property of combining with a substance as it burns. Different isotopes of an element even behave the same in chemical changes in your body.

✓ Reading Check In what cases are differences between isotopes important?

Telling Isotopes Apart

You can identify each isotope of an element by its mass number. The **mass number** is the sum of the protons and neutrons in an atom. Electrons are not included in an atom's mass number because their mass is so small that they have very little effect on the atom's total mass. Look at the boron isotope models shown in **Figure 5** to see how to calculate an atom's mass number.

Figure 5 **Isotopes of Boron**

Each of these boron isotopes has five protons. But because each has a different number of neutrons, each has a different mass number.

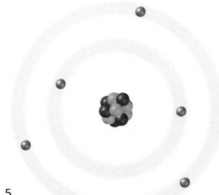

Protons: 5
Neutrons: 5
Electrons: 5
Mass number = protons + neutrons = 10

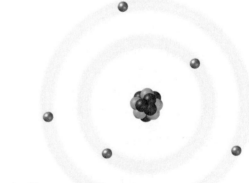

Protons: 5
Neutrons: 6
Electrons: 5
Mass number = protons + neutrons = 11

Naming Isotopes

To identify a specific isotope of an element, write the name of the element followed by a hyphen and the mass number of the isotope. A hydrogen atom with one proton and no neutrons has a mass number of 1. Its name is hydrogen-1. Hydrogen-2 has one proton and one neutron. The carbon isotope with a mass number of 12 is called carbon-12. If you know that the atomic number for carbon is 6, you can calculate the number of neutrons in carbon-12 by subtracting the atomic number from the mass number. For carbon-12, the number of neutrons is 12 − 6, or 6.

$$
\begin{array}{r}
12 \text{ Mass number} \\
- \ 6 \text{ Number of protons (atomic number)} \\
\hline
6 \text{ Number of neutrons}
\end{array}
$$

Calculating the Mass of an Element

Most elements contain a mixture of two or more isotopes. For example, all copper is composed of copper-63 atoms and copper-65 atoms. The **atomic mass** of an element is the weighted average of the masses of all the naturally occurring isotopes of that element. A weighted average accounts for the percentages of each isotope that are present. Copper, including the copper in the Statue of Liberty, shown in **Figure 6,** is 69% copper-63 and 31% copper-65. The atomic mass of copper is 63.6 amu.

Figure 6 *The copper used to make the Statue of Liberty includes both copper-63 and copper-65. Copper's atomic mass is 63.6 amu.*

atomic mass the mass of an atom expressed in atomic mass units

Atomic Mass Chlorine-35 makes up 76% of all the chlorine in nature, and chlorine-37 makes up the other 24%. What is the atomic mass of chlorine?

Step 1: Multiply the mass number of each isotope by its percentage abundance in decimal form.

$$
\begin{aligned}
(35 \times 0.76) &= 26.60 \\
(37 \times 0.24) &= 8.88
\end{aligned}
$$

Step 2: Add these amounts together to find the atomic mass.

$$
\begin{array}{r}
(35 \times 0.76) = 26.60 \\
(37 \times 0.24) = + \ 8.88 \\
\hline
35.48 \text{ amu}
\end{array}
$$

Now It's Your Turn

1. Calculate the atomic mass of boron, which occurs naturally as 20% boron-10 and 80% boron-11.

2. Calculate the atomic mass of rubidium, which occurs naturally as 72% rubidium-85 and 28% rubidium-87.

3. Calculate the atomic mass of gallium, which occurs naturally as 60% gallium-69 and 40% gallium-71.

4. Calculate the atomic mass of silver, which occurs naturally as 52% silver-107 and 48% silver-109.

5. Calculate the atomic mass of silicon, which occurs naturally as 92% silicon-28, 5% silicon-29, and 3% silicon-30.

Forces in Atoms

You have seen that atoms are made of smaller particles. But what are the *forces* (the pushes or pulls between objects) acting between these particles? Four basic forces are at work everywhere, even within the atom. These forces are gravitational force, electromagnetic force, strong force, and weak force. These forces work together to give an atom its structure and properties. Look at **Figure 7** to learn about each one.

✓ **Reading Check** What are the four basic forces at work everywhere in nature?

Figure 7 Forces in the Atom

Gravitational Force Probably the most familiar of the four forces is *gravitational force*. Gravitational force acts between all objects all the time. The amount of gravitational force between objects depends on their masses and the distance between them. Gravitational force pulls objects, such as the sun, Earth, cars, and books, toward one another. However, because the masses of particles in atoms are so small, the gravitational force within atoms is very small.

Electromagnetic Force As mentioned earlier, objects that have the same charge repel each other, while objects with opposite charge attract each other. This is due to the *electromagnetic force*. Protons and electrons are attracted to each other because they have opposite charges. The electromagnetic force holds the electrons around the nucleus.

Particles with the same charges repel each other.

Particles with opposite charges attract each other.

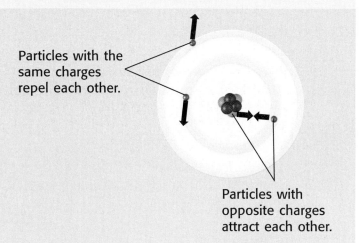

Strong Force Protons push away from one another because of the electromagnetic force. A nucleus containing two or more protons would fly apart if it were not for the *strong force*. At the close distances between protons and neutrons in the nucleus, the strong force is greater than the electromagnetic force, so the nucleus stays together.

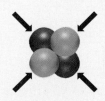

Weak Force The *weak force* is an important force in radioactive atoms. In certain unstable atoms, a neutron can change into a proton and an electron. The weak force plays a key role in this change.

Summary

- Atoms are extremely small. Ordinary-sized objects are made up of very large numbers of atoms.

- Atoms consist of a nucleus, which has protons and usually neutrons, and electrons, located in electron clouds around the nucleus.

- The number of protons in the nucleus of an atom is that atom's atomic number. All atoms of an element have the same atomic number.

- Different isotopes of an element have different numbers of neutrons in their nuclei. Isotopes of an element share most chemical and physical properties.

- The mass number of an atom is the sum of the atom's neutrons and protons.

- Atomic mass is a weighted average of the masses of natural isotopes of an element.

- The forces at work in an atom are gravitational force, electromagnetic force, strong force, and weak force.

Using Key Terms

1. Use the following terms in the same sentence: *proton*, *neutron*, and *isotope*.

Complete each of the following sentences by choosing the correct term from the word bank.

atomic mass unit	atomic number
mass number	atomic mass

2. An atom's ___ is equal to the number of protons in its nucleus.

3. An atom's ___ is equal to the weighted average of the masses of all the naturally occurring isotopes of that element.

Understanding Key Ideas

4. Which of the following particles has no electric charge?
   a. proton
   b. neutron
   c. electron
   d. ion

5. Name and describe the four forces that are at work within the nucleus of an atom.

Math Skills

6. The metal thallium occurs naturally as 30% thallium-203 and 70% thallium-205. Calculate the atomic mass of thallium.

Critical Thinking

7. **Analyzing Ideas** Why is gravitational force in the nucleus so small?

8. **Predicting Consequences** Could a nucleus of more than one proton but no neutrons exist? Explain.

Interpreting Graphics

9. Look at the two atomic models below. Do the two atoms represent different elements or different isotopes? Explain.

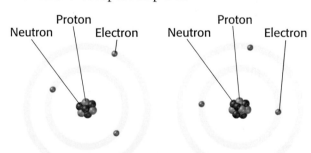

For a variety of links related to this chapter, go to www.scilinks.org

Topic: Inside the Atom; Isotopes
SciLinks code: HSM0799; HSM0820

Model-Making Lab

Made to Order

Imagine that you are an employee at the Elements-4-U Company, which custom builds elements. Your job is to construct the atomic nucleus for each element ordered by your clients. You were hired for the position because of your knowledge about what a nucleus is made of and your understanding of how isotopes of an element differ from each other. Now, it's time to put that knowledge to work!

OBJECTIVES

Build models of nuclei of certain isotopes.

Use the periodic table to determine the composition of atomic nuclei.

MATERIALS

- periodic table
- plastic-foam balls, blue, 2–3 cm in diameter (6)
- plastic-foam balls, white, 2–3 cm in diameter (4)
- toothpicks (20)

SAFETY

Procedure

1. Copy the table below onto another sheet of paper. Be sure to leave room to expand the table to include more elements.

2. Your first assignment is the nucleus of hydrogen-1. Pick up one proton (a white plastic-foam ball). Congratulations! You have built a hydrogen-1 nucleus, the simplest nucleus possible.

3. Count the number of protons and neutrons in the nucleus, and fill in rows 1 and 2 for this element in the table.

4. Use the information in rows 1 and 2 to determine the atomic number and mass number of the element. Record this information in the table.

Data Collection Table						
	Hydrogen-1	Hydrogen-2	Helium-3	Helium-4	Beryllium-9	Beryllium-10
Number of protons						
Number of neutrons						
Atomic number						
Mass number						

DO NOT WRITE IN BOOK

5 Draw a picture of your model.

6 Hydrogen-2 is an isotope of hydrogen that has one proton and one neutron. Using a strong-force connector, add a neutron to your hydrogen-1 nucleus. (Remember that in a nucleus, the protons and neutrons are held together by the strong force, which is represented in this activity by the toothpicks.) Repeat steps 3–5.

7 Helium-3 is an isotope of helium that has two protons and one neutron. Add one proton to your hydrogen-2 nucleus to create a helium-3 nucleus. Each particle should be connected to the other two particles so that they make a triangle, not a line. Protons and neutrons always form the smallest arrangement possible because the strong force pulls them together. Then, repeat steps 3–5.

8 For the next part of the lab, you will need to use information from the periodic table of the elements. Look at the illustration below. It shows the periodic table entry for carbon. You can find the atomic number of any element at the top of its entry on the periodic table. For example, the atomic number of carbon is 6.

Atomic number ⟋ **6**
C
Carbon

9 Use the information in the periodic table to build models of the following isotopes of elements: helium-4, lithium-7, beryllium-9, and beryllium-10. Remember to put the protons and neutrons as close together as possible—each particle should attach to at least two others. Repeat steps 3–5 for each isotope.

Analyze the Results

1 **Examining Data** What is the relationship between the number of protons and the atomic number?

2 **Analyzing Data** If you know the atomic number and the mass number of an isotope, how could you figure out the number of neutrons in its nucleus?

Draw Conclusions

3 **Applying Conclusions** Look up uranium on the periodic table. What is the atomic number of uranium? How many neutrons does the isotope uranium-235 have?

4 **Evaluating Models** Compare your model with the models of your classmates. How are the models similar? How are they different?

Applying Your Data

Combine your model with one that another student has made to create a single nucleus. Identify the element (and isotope) you have created.

Chapter Review

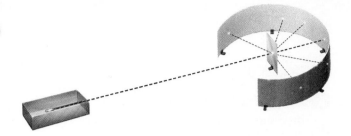

USING KEY TERMS

The statements below are false. For each statement, replace the underlined term to make a true statement.

1 <u>Electrons</u> have a positive charge.

2 All atoms of the same element contain the same number of <u>neutrons</u>.

3 <u>Protons</u> have no electrical charge.

4 The <u>atomic number</u> of an element is the number of protons and neutrons in the nucleus.

5 The <u>mass number</u> is an average of the masses of all naturally occurring isotopes of an element.

UNDERSTANDING KEY IDEAS

Multiple Choice

6 The discovery of which particle proved that the atom is not indivisible?

a. proton

b. neutron

c. electron

d. nucleus

7 How many protons does an atom with an atomic number of 23 and a mass number of 51 have?

a. 23

b. 28

c. 51

d. 74

8 In Rutherford's gold-foil experiment, Rutherford concluded that the atom is mostly empty space with a small, massive, positively charged center because

a. most of the particles passed straight through the foil.

b. some particles were slightly deflected.

c. a few particles bounced straight back.

d. All of the above

9 Which of the following determines the identity of an element?

a. atomic number

b. mass number

c. atomic mass

d. overall charge

10 Isotopes exist because atoms of the same element can have different numbers of

a. protons.

b. neutrons.

c. electrons.

d. None of the above

Short Answer

11 What force holds electrons in atoms?

12 In two or three sentences, describe Thomson's plum-pudding model of the atom.

Math Skills

13 Calculate the atomic mass of gallium, which consists of 60% gallium-69 and 40% gallium-71.

14 Calculate the number of protons, neutrons, and electrons in an atom of zirconium-90 that has no overall charge and an atomic number of 40.

CRITICAL THINKING

15 **Concept Mapping** Use the following terms to create a concept map: *atom, nucleus, protons, neutrons, electrons, isotopes, atomic number,* and *mass number.*

16 **Analyzing Processes** Particle accelerators, such as the one below, are devices that speed up charged particles in order to smash them together. Scientists use these devices to make atoms. How can scientists determine whether the atoms formed are a new element or a new isotope of a known element?

17 **Analyzing Ideas** John Dalton made a number of statements about atoms that are now known to be incorrect. Why do you think his atomic theory is still found in science textbooks?

18 **Analyzing Methods** If scientists had tried to repeat Thomson's experiment and found that they could not, would Thomson's conclusion still have been valid? Explain your answer.

INTERPRETING GRAPHICS

Use the diagrams below to answer the questions that follow.

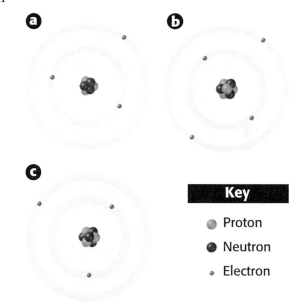

Key

- Proton
- Neutron
- Electron

19 Which diagrams represent isotopes of the same element?

20 What is the atomic number for A?

21 What is the mass number for B?

Standardized Test Preparation

Read each of the passages below. Then, answer the questions that follow each passage.

Passage 1 In the Bohr model of the atom, electrons can be found only in certain energy levels. Electrons "jump" from one level to the next level without passing through any of the regions in between. When an electron moves from one level to another, it gains or loses energy, depending on the direction of its jump. Bohr's model explained an unusual event. When electric charges pass through atoms of a gaseous element, the gas produces a glowing light, like in a neon sign. If this light is passed through a prism, a pattern of lines appears, each line having a different color. The pattern depends on the element—neon has one pattern, and helium has another. In Bohr's model, the lines are caused by electron jumps from higher to lower energy levels. Because only certain jumps are possible, electrons release energy only in certain quantities. These "packets" of energy produce the lines that are seen.

1. In the Bohr model of the atom, what limitation is placed on electrons?
   A the number of electrons in an atom
   B the electrons' being found only in certain energy levels
   C the size of electrons
   D the speed of electrons

2. What causes the colored lines that appear when the light from a gas is passed through a prism?
   F packets of energy released by electron jumps
   G electrons changing color
   H atoms of the gas exchanging electrons
   I There is not enough information to determine the answer.

Passage 2 No one has ever seen a living dinosaur, but scientists have determined the appearance of *Tyrannosaurus rex* by studying fossilized skeletons. Scientists theorize that these extinct creatures had big hind legs, small front legs, a long, whip-like tail, and a mouth full of dagger-shaped teeth. However, theories of how *T. rex* walked have been harder to develop. For many years, most scientists thought that *T. rex* plodded slowly like a big, lazy lizard. However, after studying well-preserved dinosaur tracks and noticing skeletal similarities between certain dinosaur fossils and living creatures like the ostrich, many scientists now theorize that *T. rex* could turn on the speed. Some scientists estimate that *T. rex* had bursts of speed of 32 km/h (20 mi/h)!

1. According to this passage, where does most of what we know about the appearance of *Tyrannosaurus rex* come from?
   A fossilized skeletons
   B dinosaur tracks
   C living organisms such as the ostrich
   D living specimens of *T. rex*

2. How did scientists conclude that *T. rex* could probably move very quickly?
   F They measured the speed at which it could run.
   G They compared fossilized *T. rex* tracks with *T. rex* skeletons.
   H They studied dinosaur tracks and noted similarities between ostrich skeletons and *T. rex* skeletons.
   I They measured the speed at which ostriches could run.

Use the diagram of an atom below to answer the questions that follow.

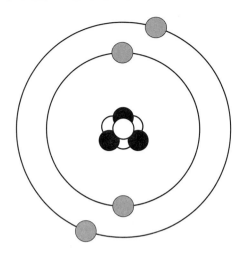

1. The black circles in the center of the model represent neutrons. What do the white circles in the center represent?

A electrons

B protons

C nuclei

D atoms

2. What is the mass number of the atom shown in the model?

F 3

G 7

H 9

I 11

3. What is the overall charge of the atom shown in the model?

A +2

B +1

C 0

D −1

Read each question below, and choose the best answer.

1. Aimee, Mari, and Brooke are 163 cm, 171 cm, and 175 cm tall. Which of the following measurements is a reasonable average height of these three friends?

A 170 cm

B 175 cm

C 255 cm

D 509 cm

2. A certain school has 40 classrooms. Most of the classrooms have 25 to 30 students. Which of the following is a reasonable estimate of the number of students that go to this school?

F 40 students

G 100 students

H 1,100 students

I 2,000 students

3. Jenna is setting up a fish tank in her room. The tank is the shape of a rectangular prism. The height of the tank is 38 cm, the width is 23 cm, and the length is 62 cm. The tank is filled with water to a point that is 7 cm from the top. How much water is in the tank?

A 44,206 cm^3

B 48,070 cm^3

C 54,188 cm^3

D 64,170 cm^3

4. Which of the following is equal to 8^5?

F $8 + 8 + 8 + 8 + 8$

G $5 \times 5 \times 5 \times 5 \times 5 \times 5 \times 5 \times 5$

H 5×8

I $8 \times 8 \times 8 \times 8 \times 8$

Science in Action

Weird Science

Mining on the Moon?

Since the end of the Apollo moon missions in 1972, no one has set foot on the surface of the moon. But today, an isotope of helium known as *helium-3* is fueling new interest in returning to the moon. Some scientists speculate that helium-3 can be used as a safe and nonpolluting fuel for a new kind of power plant. Helium-3 is very rare on Earth, but a huge amount of the isotope exists on the surface of the moon. But how can helium-3 be brought to Earth? Some researchers imagine a robotic lunar mining operation that will harvest the helium-3 and transport it to Earth.

Language Arts ACTIVITY

WRITING SKILL Write a paragraph in which you rephrase the information above in your own words. Be sure to include what helium-3 is, where it can be found, and how it could be used.

Scientific Discoveries

Modern Alchemy

Hundreds of years ago, many people thought that if you treated lead with certain chemicals, it would turn into gold. People called *alchemists* often spent their whole lives trying to find a way to make gold from other metals, such as lead. We now know that the methods alchemists tried to change one element to another did not work. But in the 20th century, scientists learned that you really could change one element to another! In a nuclear reaction, small particles can be collided with atomic nuclei. This process makes the nuclei split apart to form two nuclei of different elements.

Math ACTIVITY

If you split apart an atom of lead (atomic number = 82) and one of the atoms left was gold (atomic number = 79), what would be the atomic number of the other atom that resulted from this change?

Melissa Franklin

Experimental Physicist In the course of a single day, you could find experimental physicist Melissa Franklin running a huge drill or showing her lab to a 10-year-old child. You could see her putting together a huge piece of electronic equipment or even telling a joke. Then you'd see her really get down to business—studying the smallest particles of matter in the universe.

"I am trying to understand the forces that describe how everything in the world moves—especially the smallest things," Franklin explains. Franklin and her team helped discover a particle called the top quark. (Quarks are the tiny particles that make up protons and neutrons.) "You can understand the ideas without having to be a math genius," Franklin says. "Anyone can have ideas," she says, "absolutely anyone." Franklin also has some advice for young people interested in physics. "Go and bug people at the local university. Just call up a physics person and say, 'Can I come visit you for a couple of hours?' Kids do that with me, and it's really fun."

Social Studies ACTIVITY

WRITING SKILL Find out about an experimental physicist who made an important discovery. Write a one-page report about how that discovery affected the ideas of other scientists.

To learn more about these Science in Action topics, visit **go.hrw.com** and type in the keyword **HP5ATSF.**

Current Science

Check out Current Science® articles related to this chapter by visiting go.hrw.com. Just type in the keyword **HP5CS11.**

The Periodic Table

The Big Idea

Elements are organized on the periodic table according to their properties.

About the PHOTO

You already know or have heard about elements on the periodic table, such as oxygen, carbon, and neon. Neon gas was discovered in 1898. In 1902, a French engineer, chemist, and inventor named Georges Claude made the first neon lamp. In 1910, Claude made the first neon sign, and in 1923, he introduced neon signs to the United States. Now, artists such as Eric Ehlenberger use glass and neon to create interesting works of art, such as these neon jellyfish.

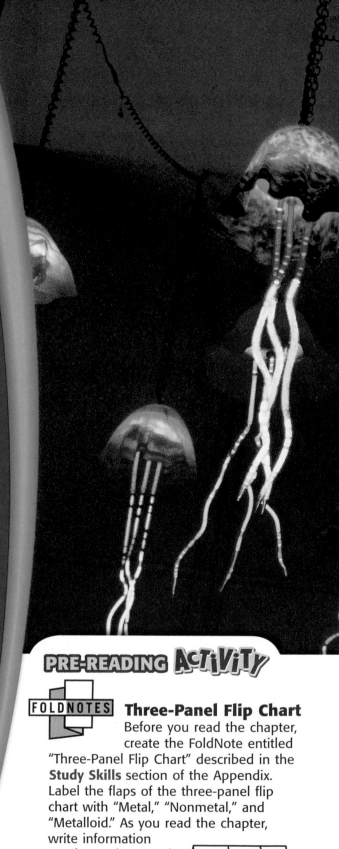

PRE-READING ACTIVITY

FOLDNOTES **Three-Panel Flip Chart**
Before you read the chapter, create the FoldNote entitled "Three-Panel Flip Chart" described in the **Study Skills** section of the Appendix. Label the flaps of the three-panel flip chart with "Metal," "Nonmetal," and "Metalloid." As you read the chapter, write information you learn about each category under the appropriate flap.

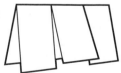

START-UP ACTIVITY

Placement Pattern

In this activity, you will identify the pattern your teacher used to create a new classroom seating arrangement.

Procedure

1. Draw a seating chart for the new classroom arrangement that your teacher gave to you. Write the name of each of your classmates in the place on the chart that corresponds to his or her seat.

2. Write information about yourself, such as your name, date of birth, hair color, and height, in the space that represents you on the chart.

3. Gather the same information about the people near you, and write it in the spaces on the chart.

Analysis

1. From the information you gathered, identify a pattern that might explain the order of people in the chart. Collect more information if needed.

2. Test your pattern by gathering information from a person you did not talk to before.

3. If the new information does not support your pattern, reanalyze your data and collect more information to determine another pattern.

Arranging the Elements

Suppose you went to the video store and all the videos were mixed together. How could you tell the comedies from the action movies? If the videos were not arranged in a pattern, you wouldn't know what kind of movie you had chosen!

Scientists in the early 1860s had a similar problem. At that time, scientists knew some of the properties of more than 60 elements. However, no one had organized the elements according to these properties. Organizing the elements according to their properties would help scientists understand how elements interact with each other.

Discovering a Pattern

Dmitri Mendeleev (duh MEE tree MEN duh LAY uhf), a Russian chemist, discovered a pattern to the elements in 1869. First, he wrote the names and properties of the elements on cards. Then, he arranged his cards, as shown in **Figure 1,** by different properties, such as density, appearance, and melting point. After much thought, he arranged the elements in order of increasing atomic mass. When he did so, a pattern appeared.

✓ Reading Check How had Mendeleev arranged elements when he noticed a pattern? (*See the Appendix for answers to Reading Checks.*)

Figure 1 By playing "chemical solitaire" on long train rides, Mendeleev organized the elements according to their properties.

Table 1 Properties of Germanium

	Mendeleev's predictions (1869)	Actual properties
Atomic mass	70	72.6
Density*	5.5 g/cm³	5.3 g/cm³
Appearance	dark gray metal	gray metal
Melting point*	high melting point	937°C

* at room temperature and pressure

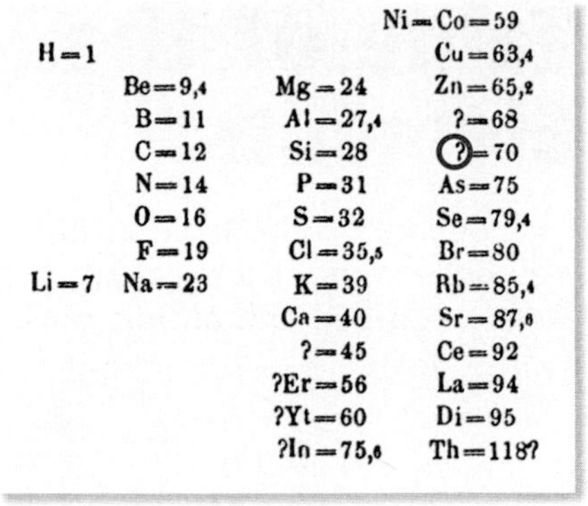

Periodic Properties of the Elements

Mendeleev saw that when the elements were arranged in order of increasing atomic mass, those that had similar properties occurred in a repeating pattern. That is, the pattern was periodic. **Periodic** means "happening at regular intervals." The days of the week are periodic. They repeat in the same order every 7 days. Similarly, Mendeleev found that the elements' properties followed a pattern that repeated every seven elements. His table became known as the *periodic table of the elements.*

Predicting Properties of Missing Elements

Figure 2 shows part of Mendeleev's first try at arranging the elements. The question marks show gaps in the pattern. Mendeleev predicted that elements yet to be found would fill these gaps. He used the pattern he found to predict their properties. **Table 1** compares his predictions for one missing element—germanium—with its actual properties. By 1886, all of the gaps had been filled. His predictions were right.

Changing the Arrangement

A few elements' properties did not fit the pattern in Mendeleev's table. Mendeleev thought that more-accurate atomic masses would fix these flaws in his table. But new atomic mass measurements showed that the masses he had used were correct. In 1914, Henry Moseley (MOHZ lee), a British scientist, determined the number of protons—the atomic number—in an atom. All elements fit the pattern in Mendeleev's periodic table when they were arranged by atomic number.

Look at the periodic table on the next two pages. All of the more than 30 elements discovered since 1914 follow the periodic law. The **periodic law** states that the repeating chemical and physical properties of elements change periodically with the elements' atomic numbers.

✓ Reading Check What property is used to arrange elements in the periodic table?

Figure 2 *Mendeleev used question marks to mark some elements that he thought would be found later.*

periodic describes something that occurs or repeats at regular intervals

periodic law the law that states that the repeating chemical and physical properties of elements change periodically with the atomic numbers of the elements

CONNECTION TO Language Arts

WRITING SKILL **Hidden Help** You may be asked to memorize some of the chemical symbols. A story or poem that uses the symbols might be helpful. In your **science journal,** write a short story, poem, or just a few sentences in which the words correspond to and bring to mind the chemical symbols of the first 20 elements.

Periodic Table of the Elements

Each square on the table includes an element's name, chemical symbol, atomic number, and atomic mass.

The color of the chemical symbol indicates the physical state at room temperature. Carbon is a solid.

6	— Atomic number
C	— Chemical symbol
Carbon	— Element name
12.0	— Atomic mass

The background color indicates the type of element. Carbon is a nonmetal.

Background
- Metals
- Metalloids
- Nonmetals

Chemical symbol
- Solid
- Liquid
- Gas

Period 1

1
H
Hydrogen
1.0

	Group 1	Group 2	Group 3	Group 4	Group 5	Group 6	Group 7	Group 8	Group 9
Period 2	3 **Li** Lithium 6.9	4 **Be** Beryllium 9.0							
Period 3	11 **Na** Sodium 23.0	12 **Mg** Magnesium 24.3							
Period 4	19 **K** Potassium 39.1	20 **Ca** Calcium 40.1	21 **Sc** Scandium 45.0	22 **Ti** Titanium 47.9	23 **V** Vanadium 50.9	24 **Cr** Chromium 52.0	25 **Mn** Manganese 54.9	26 **Fe** Iron 55.8	27 **Co** Cobalt 58.9
Period 5	37 **Rb** Rubidium 85.5	38 **Sr** Strontium 87.6	39 **Y** Yttrium 88.9	40 **Zr** Zirconium 91.2	41 **Nb** Niobium 92.9	42 **Mo** Molybdenum 95.9	43 **Tc** Technetium (98)	44 **Ru** Ruthenium 101.1	45 **Rh** Rhodium 102.9
Period 6	55 **Cs** Cesium 132.9	56 **Ba** Barium 137.3	57 **La** Lanthanum 138.9	72 **Hf** Hafnium 178.5	73 **Ta** Tantalum 180.9	74 **W** Tungsten 183.8	75 **Re** Rhenium 186.2	76 **Os** Osmium 190.2	77 **Ir** Iridium 192.2
Period 7	87 **Fr** Francium (223)	88 **Ra** Radium (226)	89 **Ac** Actinium (227)	104 **Rf** Rutherfordium (261)	105 **Db** Dubnium (262)	106 **Sg** Seaborgium (266)	107 **Bh** Bohrium (264)	108 **Hs** Hassium (277)	109 **Mt** Meitnerium (268)

A row of elements is called a *period*.

A column of elements is called a *group* or *family*.

Values in parentheses are the mass numbers of those radioactive elements' most stable or most common isotopes.

These elements are placed below the table to allow the table to be narrower.

Lanthanides

58 **Ce** Cerium 140.1	59 **Pr** Praseodymium 140.9	60 **Nd** Neodymium 144.2	61 **Pm** Promethium (145)	62 **Sm** Samarium 150.4

Actinides

90 **Th** Thorium 232.0	91 **Pa** Protactinium 231.0	92 **U** Uranium 238.0	93 **Np** Neptunium (237)	94 **Pu** Plutonium (244)

Topic: **Periodic Table**
Go To: **go.hrw.com**
Keyword: **HN0 PERIODIC**
Visit the HRW Web site for
updates on the periodic table.

This zigzag line reminds you where the metals, nonmetals, and metalloids are.

Group 10	Group 11	Group 12	Group 13	Group 14	Group 15	Group 16	Group 17	Group 18
								2 **He** Helium 4.0
			5 **B** Boron 10.8	6 **C** Carbon 12.0	7 **N** Nitrogen 14.0	8 **O** Oxygen 16.0	9 **F** Fluorine 19.0	10 **Ne** Neon 20.2
			13 **Al** Aluminum 27.0	14 **Si** Silicon 28.1	15 **P** Phosphorus 31.0	16 **S** Sulfur 32.1	17 **Cl** Chlorine 35.5	18 **Ar** Argon 39.9
28 **Ni** Nickel 58.7	29 **Cu** Copper 63.5	30 **Zn** Zinc 65.4	31 **Ga** Gallium 69.7	32 **Ge** Germanium 72.6	33 **As** Arsenic 74.9	34 **Se** Selenium 79.0	35 **Br** Bromine 79.9	36 **Kr** Krypton 83.8
46 **Pd** Palladium 106.4	47 **Ag** Silver 107.9	48 **Cd** Cadmium 112.4	49 **In** Indium 114.8	50 **Sn** Tin 118.7	51 **Sb** Antimony 121.8	52 **Te** Tellurium 127.6	53 **I** Iodine 126.9	54 **Xe** Xenon 131.3
78 **Pt** Platinum 195.1	79 **Au** Gold 197.0	80 **Hg** Mercury 200.6	81 **Tl** Thallium 204.4	82 **Pb** Lead 207.2	83 **Bi** Bismuth 209.0	84 **Po** Polonium (209)	85 **At** Astatine (210)	86 **Rn** Radon (222)
110 **Ds** Darmstadtium (281)	111 **Uuu** Unununium (272)	112 **Uub** Ununbium (285)	113 **Uut** Ununtrium (284)	114 **Uuq** Ununquadium (289)	115 **Uup** Ununpentium (288)			

The discovery of elements 113, 114, and 115 has been reported but not confirmed.

The names and three-letter symbols of elements are temporary. They are based on the atomic numbers of the elements. Official names and symbols will be approved by an international committee of scientists.

63 **Eu** Europium 152.0	64 **Gd** Gadolinium 157.2	65 **Tb** Terbium 158.9	66 **Dy** Dysprosium 162.5	67 **Ho** Holmium 164.9	68 **Er** Erbium 167.3	69 **Tm** Thulium 168.9	70 **Yb** Ytterbium 173.0	71 **Lu** Lutetium 175.0
95 **Am** Americium (243)	96 **Cm** Curium (247)	97 **Bk** Berkelium (247)	98 **Cf** Californium (251)	99 **Es** Einsteinium (252)	100 **Fm** Fermium (257)	101 **Md** Mendelevium (258)	102 **No** Nobelium (259)	103 **Lr** Lawrencium (262)

The Periodic Table and Classes of Elements

At first glance, you might think studying the periodic table is like trying to explore a thick jungle without a guide—you can easily get lost! However, the table itself contains a lot of information that will help you along the way.

Elements are classified as metals, nonmetals, and metalloids, according to their properties. The number of electrons in the outer energy level of an atom is one characteristic that helps determine which category an element belongs in. The zigzag line on the periodic table can help you recognize which elements are metals, which are nonmetals, and which are metalloids.

Metals

Most elements are metals. Metals are found to the left of the zigzag line on the periodic table. Atoms of most metals have few electrons in their outer energy level. Most metals are solid at room temperature. Mercury, however, is a liquid at room temperature. Some additional information on properties shared by most metals is shown in **Figure 3.**

✓ **Reading Check** What are four properties shared by most metals?

Figure 3 **Properties of Metals**

Metals tend to be **shiny.** You can see a reflection in a mirror because light reflects off the shiny surface of a thin layer of silver behind the glass.

Most metals are **ductile,** which means that they can be drawn into thin wires. All metals are **good conductors of electric current.** The wires in the electrical devices in your home are made of copper.

Most metals are **malleable,** which means that they can be flattened with a hammer and will not shatter. Aluminum is flattened into sheets to make cans and foil.

Most metals are **good conductors of thermal energy.** This iron griddle conducts thermal energy from a stove top to cook your favorite foods.

Figure 4 Properties of Nonmetals

Nonmetals are **not malleable or ductile.** In fact, solid nonmetals, such as carbon in the graphite of the pencil lead, are brittle and will break or shatter when hit with a hammer.

Sulfur, like most nonmetals, is **not shiny.**

Nonmetals are **poor conductors of thermal energy and electric current.** If the gap in a spark plug is too wide, the nonmetals nitrogen and oxygen in the air will stop the spark and a car's engine will not run.

Nonmetals

Nonmetals are found to the right of the zigzag line on the periodic table. Atoms of most nonmetals have an almost complete set of electrons in their outer level. Atoms of the elements in Group 18, the noble gases, have a complete set of electrons. More than half of the nonmetals are gases at room temperature. Many properties of nonmetals are the opposite of the properties of metals, as shown in **Figure 4.**

Metalloids

Metalloids, also called *semiconductors,* are the elements that border the zigzag line on the periodic table. Atoms of metalloids have about half of a complete set of electrons in their outer energy level. Metalloids have some properties of metals and some properties of nonmetals, as shown in **Figure 5.**

MATH PRACTICE

Percentages

Elements are classified as metals, nonmetals, and metalloids. Use the periodic table to determine the percentage of elements in each of the three categories.

Figure 5 Properties of Metalloids

Tellurium is **shiny,** but it is **brittle** and can easily be smashed into a powder.

Boron is almost as **hard** as diamond, but it is also **very brittle.** At high temperatures, it is a **good conductor of electric current.**

period in chemistry, a horizontal row of elements in the periodic table

group a vertical column of elements in the periodic table; elements in a group share chemical properties

Decoding the Periodic Table

The periodic table may seem to be in code. In a way, it is. But the colors and symbols will help you decode the table.

Each Element Is Identified by a Chemical Symbol

Each square on the periodic table includes an element's name, chemical symbol, atomic number, and atomic mass. The names of the elements come from many sources. Some elements, such as mendelevium, are named after scientists. Others, such as californium, are named after places. Some element names vary by country. But the chemical symbols are the same worldwide. For most elements, the chemical symbol has one or two letters. The first letter is always capitalized. Any other letter is always lowercase. The newest elements have temporary three-letter symbols.

Rows Are Called *Periods*

Each horizontal row of elements (from left to right) on the periodic table is called a **period.** Look at Period 4 in **Figure 6.** The physical and chemical properties of elements in a row follow a repeating, or periodic, pattern as you move across the period. Properties such as conductivity and reactivity change gradually from left to right in each period.

Columns Are Called *Groups*

Each vertical column of elements (from top to bottom) on the periodic table is called a **group.** Elements in the same group often have similar chemical and physical properties. For this reason, a group is also called a *family*.

✓ **Reading Check** Why is a group sometimes called a family?

Figure 6 *As you move from left to right across a row, the elements become less metallic.*

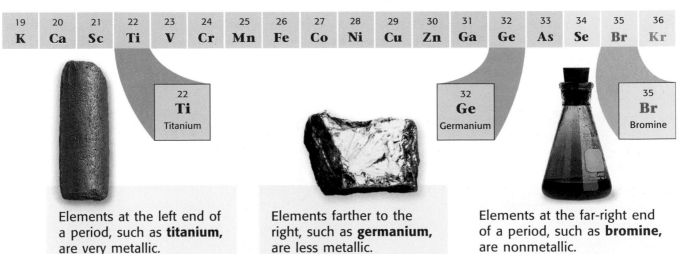

Elements at the left end of a period, such as **titanium,** are very metallic.

Elements farther to the right, such as **germanium,** are less metallic.

Elements at the far-right end of a period, such as **bromine,** are nonmetallic.

Summary

- Mendeleev developed the first periodic table by listing the elements in order of increasing atomic mass. He used his table to predict that elements with certain properties would be discovered later.
- Properties of elements repeat in a regular, or periodic, pattern.
- Moseley rearranged the elements in order of increasing atomic number.
- The periodic law states that the repeating chemical and physical properties of elements relate to and depend on elements' atomic numbers.

- Elements in the periodic table are classified as metals, nonmetals, and metalloids.
- Each element has a chemical symbol.
- A horizontal row of elements is called a *period*.
- Physical and chemical properties of elements change across each period.
- A vertical column of elements is called a *group* or *family*.
- Elements in a group usually have similar properties.

Using Key Terms

1. In your own words, write a definition for the term *periodic*.

Understanding Key Ideas

2. Which of the following elements should be the best conductor of electric current?
   a. germanium
   b. sulfur
   c. aluminum
   d. helium

3. Compare a period and a group on the periodic table.

4. What property did Mendeleev use to position the elements on the periodic table?

5. State the periodic law.

Critical Thinking

6. **Identifying Relationships** An atom that has 117 protons in its nucleus has not yet been made. Once this atom is made, to which group will element 117 belong? Explain your answer.

7. **Applying Concepts** Are the properties of sodium, Na, more like the properties of lithium, Li, or magnesium, Mg? Explain your answer.

Interpreting Graphics

8. The image below shows part of a periodic table. Compare the image below with the similar part of the periodic table in your book.

	1			
1	1 H 1.0079 水素			
2	3 Li 6.941 リチウム	4 Be 9.01218 ベリリウム		
3	11 Na 22.98977 ナトリウム	12 Mg 24.305 マグネシウム		
4	19 K	20 Ca	21 Sc	22 Ti

Grouping the Elements

You probably know a family with several members who look a lot alike. The elements in a family or group in the periodic table often—but not always—have similar properties.

The properties of the elements in a group are similar because the atoms of the elements have the same number of electrons in their outer energy level. Atoms will often take, give, or share electrons with other atoms in order to have a complete set of electrons in their outer energy level. Elements whose atoms undergo such processes are called *reactive* and can combine to form compounds.

What You Will Learn

● Explain why elements in a group often have similar properties.

● Describe the properties of the elements in the groups of the periodic table.

Vocabulary

alkali metal
alkaline-earth metal
halogen
noble gas

READING STRATEGY

Paired Summarizing Read this section silently. In pairs, take turns summarizing the material. Stop to discuss ideas that seem confusing.

Although the element hydrogen appears above the alkali metals on the periodic table, it is not considered a member of Group 1. It will be described separately at the end of this section.

Group 1: Alkali Metals

3 **Li** Lithium	**Group contains:** metals **Electrons in the outer level:** 1 **Reactivity:** very reactive **Other shared properties:** softness; color of silver; shininess; low density
11 **Na** Sodium	
19 **K** Potassium	
37 **Rb** Rubidium	
55 **Cs** Cesium	
87 **Fr** Francium	

Alkali metals (AL kuh LIE MET uhlz) are elements in Group 1 of the periodic table. They share physical and chemical properties, as shown in **Figure 1.** Alkali metals are the most reactive metals because their atoms can easily give away the one outer-level electron. Pure alkali metals are often stored in oil. The oil keeps them from reacting with water and oxygen in the air. Alkali metals are so reactive that in nature they are found only combined with other elements. Compounds formed from alkali metals have many uses. For example, sodium chloride (table salt) is used to flavor your food. Potassium bromide is used in photography.

Figure 1   **Properties of Alkali Metals**

Sodium

Sodium

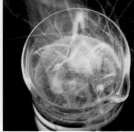
Potassium

▲ Alkali metals are soft enough to be cut with a knife.

▲ Alkali metals react with water to form hydrogen gas.

Group 2: Alkaline-Earth Metals

4 **Be** Beryllium	**Group contains:** metals **Electrons in the outer level:** 2 **Reactivity:** very reactive but less reactive than alkali metals **Other shared properties:** color of silver; higher densities than alkali metals
12 **Mg** Magnesium	

4
Be
Beryllium

12
Mg
Magnesium

20
Ca
Calcium

38
Sr
Strontium

56
Ba
Barium

88
Ra
Radium

Group contains: metals
Electrons in the outer level: 2
Reactivity: very reactive but less reactive than alkali metals
Other shared properties: color of silver; higher densities than alkali metals

Alkaline-earth metals (AL kuh LIEN UHRTH MET uhlz) are less reactive than alkali metals are. Atoms of alkaline-earth metals have two outer-level electrons. It is more difficult for atoms to give two electrons than to give one when joining with other atoms. Group 2 elements and their compounds have many uses. For example, magnesium can be mixed with other metals to make low-density materials used in airplanes. And compounds of calcium are found in cement, chalk, and even you, as shown in **Figure 2.**

Figure 2 *Calcium, an alkaline-earth metal, is an important part of a compound that keeps your bones and teeth healthy.*

Groups 3–12: Transition Metals

21 **Sc**	22 **Ti**	23 **V**	24 **Cr**	25 **Mn**	26 **Fe**	27 **Co**	28 **Ni**	29 **Cu**	30 **Zn**
39 **Y**	40 **Zr**	41 **Nb**	42 **Mo**	43 **Tc**	44 **Ru**	45 **Rh**	46 **Pd**	47 **Ag**	48 **Cd**
57 **La**	72 **Hf**	73 **Ta**	74 **W**	75 **Re**	76 **Os**	77 **Ir**	78 **Pt**	79 **Au**	80 **Hg**
89 **Ac**	104 **Rf**	105 **Db**	106 **Sg**	107 **Bh**	108 **Hs**	109 **Mt**	110 **Ds**	111 **Uuu**	112 **Uub**

Group contains: metals
Electrons in the outer level: 1 or 2
Reactivity: less reactive than alkaline-earth metals
Other shared properties: shininess; good conductors of thermal energy and electric current; higher densities and melting points than elements in Groups 1 and 2 (except for mercury)

alkali metal one of the elements of Group 1 of the periodic table (lithium, sodium, potassium, rubidium, cesium, and francium)

alkaline-earth metal one of the elements of Group 2 of the periodic table (beryllium, magnesium, calcium, strontium, barium, and radium)

Groups 3–12 do not have individual names. Instead, all of these groups are called *transition metals.* The atoms of transition metals do not give away their electrons as easily as atoms of the Group 1 and Group 2 metals do. So, transition metals are less reactive than alkali metals and alkaline-earth metals are.

✓ Reading Check Why are alkali metals more reactive than transition metals are? (*See the Appendix for answers to Reading Checks.*)

Figure 3 Properties of Transition Metals

Mercury is used in thermometers. Unlike the other transition metals, mercury is liquid at room temperature.

Many transition metals—but not all—are silver colored! This **gold** ring proves it!

Some transition metals, such as **titanium** in the artificial hip at right, are not very reactive. But others, such as **iron,** are reactive. The iron in the steel trowel on the left has reacted to form rust.

Properties of Transition Metals

The properties of the transition metals vary widely, as shown in **Figure 3.** But, because these elements are metals, they share the properties of metals. Transition metals tend to be shiny and to conduct thermal energy and electric current well.

Lanthanides and Actinides

Some transition metals from Periods 6 and 7 appear in two rows at the bottom of the periodic table to keep the table from being too wide. The elements in each row tend to have similar properties. Elements in the first row follow lanthanum and are called *lanthanides.* The lanthanides are shiny, reactive metals. Some of these elements are used to make steel. An important use of a compound of one lanthanide element is shown in **Figure 4.**

Elements in the second row follow actinium and are called *actinides.* All atoms of actinides are radioactive, or unstable. The atoms of a radioactive element can change into atoms of another element. Elements listed after plutonium, element 94, do not occur in nature. They are made in laboratories. Very small amounts of americium (AM uhr ISH ee uhm), element 95, are used in some smoke detectors.

✓ *Reading Check* Are lanthanides and actinides transition metals?

Figure 4 *Do you see red? The color red appears on a computer monitor because of a compound formed from europium that coats the back of the screen.*

57
La
Lanthanum

89
Ac
Actinium

Lanthanides	58 Ce	59 Pr	60 Nd	61 Pm	62 Sm	63 Eu	64 Gd	65 Tb	66 Dy	67 Ho	68 Er	69 Tm	70 Yb	71 Lu
Actinides	90 Th	91 Pa	92 U	93 Np	94 Pu	95 Am	96 Cm	97 Bk	98 Cf	99 Es	100 Fm	101 Md	102 No	103 Lr

Group 13: Boron Group

5 **B** Boron	**Group contains:** one metalloid and five metals **Electrons in the outer level:** 3 **Reactivity:** reactive **Other shared properties:** solids at room temperature
13 **Al** Aluminum	
31 **Ga** Gallium	
49 **In** Indium	
81 **Tl** Thallium	
113 **Uut** Ununtrium	

The most common element from Group 13 is aluminum. In fact, aluminum is the most abundant metal in Earth's crust. Until the 1880s, however, aluminum was considered a precious metal because the process used to make pure aluminum was very expensive. During the 1850s and 1860s, Emperor Napoleon III of France used aluminum dinnerware because aluminum was more valuable than gold.

Today, the process of making pure aluminum is easier and less expensive than it was in the 1800s. Aluminum is now an important metal used in making aircraft parts. Aluminum is also used to make lightweight automobile parts, foil, cans, and siding.

Like the other elements in the boron group, aluminum is reactive. Why can it be used in so many things? A thin layer of aluminum oxide quickly forms on aluminum's surface when aluminum reacts with oxygen in the air. This layer prevents further reaction of the aluminum.

Group 14: Carbon Group

6 **C** Carbon	**Group contains:** one nonmetal, two metalloids, and three metals **Electrons in the outer level:** 4 **Reactivity:** varies among the elements **Other shared properties:** solids at room temperature
14 **Si** Silicon	
32 **Ge** Germanium	
50 **Sn** Tin	
82 **Pb** Lead	
114 **Uuq** Ununquadium	

The nonmetal carbon can be found uncombined in nature, as shown in **Figure 5.** Carbon also forms a wide variety of compounds. Some of these compounds, such as proteins, fats, and carbohydrates, are necessary for living things on Earth.

The metalloids silicon and germanium, also in Group 14, are used to make computer chips. The metal tin is useful because it is not very reactive. For example, a tin can is really made of steel coated with tin. Because the tin is less reactive than the steel is, the tin keeps the iron in the steel from rusting.

✓ Reading Check What metalloids from Group 14 are used to make computer chips?

Figure 5 *Diamond and soot have very different properties, yet both are natural forms of carbon.*

Diamond is the hardest material known. It is used as a jewel and on cutting tools, such as saws, drills, and files.

Soot is formed from burning oil, coal, and wood and is used as a pigment in paints and crayons.

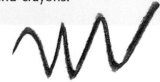

Group 15: Nitrogen Group

7 **N** Nitrogen	
15 **P** Phosphorus	
33 **As** Arsenic	
51 **Sb** Antimony	
83 **Bi** Bismuth	
115 **Uup** Ununpentium	

Group contains: two nonmetals, two metalloids, and two metals
Electrons in the outer level: 5
Reactivity: varies among the elements
Other shared properties: solids at room temperature (except for nitrogen)

Nitrogen, which is a gas at room temperature, makes up about 80% of the air you breathe. Nitrogen removed from air can be reacted with hydrogen to make ammonia for fertilizers.

Although nitrogen is not very reactive, phosphorus is extremely reactive, as shown in **Figure 6.** In fact, in nature phosphorus is only found combined with other elements.

Figure 6 *Simply striking a match on the side of this box causes chemicals on the match to react with phosphorus on the box and begin to burn.*

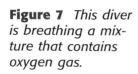

INTERNET ACTIVITY

For another activity related to this chapter, go to **go.hrw.com** and type in the keyword **HP5PRTW.**

Group 16: Oxygen Group

8 **O** Oxygen	
16 **S** Sulfur	
34 **Se** Selenium	
52 **Te** Tellurium	
84 **Po** Polonium	

Group contains: three nonmetals, one metalloid, and one metal
Electrons in the outer level: 6
Reactivity: Reactive
Other shared properties: All but oxygen are solid at room temperature.

Oxygen makes up about 20% of air. Oxygen is necessary for substances to burn. Oxygen is also important to most living things, such as the diver in **Figure 7.** Sulfur is another commonly found member of Group 16. Sulfur can be found as a yellow solid in nature. It is used to make sulfuric acid, the most widely used compound in the chemical industry.

✓ Reading Check Which gases from Groups 15 and 16 make up most of the air you breathe?

Figure 7 *This diver is breathing a mixture that contains oxygen gas.*

Figure 8 Physical Properties of Some Halogens

Chlorine is a yellowish green gas.

Bromine is a dark red liquid.

Iodine is a dark gray solid.

Group 17: Halogens

9	
F	
Fluorine	

17	
Cl	
Chlorine	

35	
Br	
Bromine	

53	
I	
Iodine	

85	
At	
Astatine	

Group contains: nonmetals
Electrons in the outer level: 7
Reactivity: very reactive
Other shared properties: poor conductors of electric current; violent reactions with alkali metals to form salts; never in uncombined form in nature

Halogens (HAL oh juhnz) are very reactive nonmetals because their atoms need to gain only one electron to have a complete outer level. The atoms of halogens combine readily with other atoms, especially metals, to gain that missing electron. The reaction of a halogen with a metal makes a salt, such as sodium chloride. Both chlorine and iodine are used as disinfectants. Chlorine is used to treat water. Iodine mixed with alcohol is used in hospitals.

Although the chemical properties of the halogens are similar, the physical properties are quite different, as shown in **Figure 8.**

halogen one of the elements of Group 17 of the periodic table (fluorine, chlorine, bromine, iodine, and astatine); halogens combine with most metals to form salts

CONNECTION TO Biology

Water Treatment Chlorine has been used to treat drinking water since the early 20th century. Chlorinating water helps protect people from many diseases by killing the organisms in water that cause the diseases. But there is much more to water treatment than just adding chlorine. Research how a water treatment plant purifies water for your use. Construct a model of a treatment plant. Use labels to describe the role of each part of the plant in treating the water you use each day.

ACTIVITY

Group 18: Noble Gases

2 **He** Helium	**Group contains:** nonmetals **Electrons in the outer level:** 8 (except helium, which has 2) **Reactivity:** unreactive **Other shared properties:** colorless, odorless gases at room temperature
10 **Ne** Neon	
18 **Ar** Argon	
36 **Kr** Krypton	
54 **Xe** Xenon	
86 **Rn** Radon	

Figure 9 *In addition to neon, other noble gases can be used to make "neon" lights.*

noble gas one of the elements of Group 18 of the periodic table (helium, neon, argon, krypton, xenon, and radon); noble gases are unreactive

Noble gases are unreactive nonmetals and are in Group 18 of the periodic table. The atoms of these elements have a full set of electrons in their outer level. So, they do not need to lose or gain any electrons. Under normal conditions, they do not react with other elements. Earth's atmosphere is almost 1% argon. But all the noble gases are found in small amounts.

The unreactivity of the noble gases makes them useful. For example, ordinary light bulbs last longer when they are filled with argon. Because argon is unreactive, it does not react with the metal filament in the light bulb even when the filament gets hot. A more reactive gas might react with the filament, causing the light to burn out. The low density of helium makes blimps and weather balloons float. Another popular use of noble gases is shown in **Figure 9.**

✓ Reading Check Why are noble gases unreactive?

Hydrogen

1 **H** Hydrogen	**Electrons in the outer level:** 1 **Reactivity:** reactive **Other properties:** colorless, odorless gas at room temperature; low density; explosive reactions with oxygen

The properties of hydrogen do not match the properties of any single group, so hydrogen is set apart from the other elements in the table. Hydrogen is above Group 1 because atoms of the alkali metals also have only one electron in their outer level. Atoms of hydrogen can give away one electron when they join with other atoms. However, the physical properties of hydrogen are more like those of nonmetals than those of metals. So, hydrogen really is in a group of its own. Hydrogen is found in stars. In fact, it is the most abundant element in the universe. Its reactive nature makes it useful as a fuel in rockets, as shown in **Figure 10.**

Figure 10 *Hydrogen reacts violently with oxygen. The hot water vapor that forms as a result of this reaction helps guide the space shuttle into orbit.*

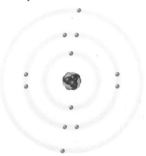

Summary

- Alkali metals (Group 1) are the most reactive metals. Atoms of the alkali metals have one electron in their outer level.

- Alkaline-earth metals (Group 2) are less reactive than the alkali metals are. Atoms of the alkaline-earth metals have two electrons in their outer level.

- Transition metals (Groups 3–12) include most of the well-known metals and the lanthanides and actinides.

- Groups 13–16 contain the metalloids and some metals and nonmetals.

- Halogens (Group 17) are very reactive non-metals. Atoms of the halogens have seven electrons in their outer level.

- Noble gases (Group 18) are unreactive nonmetals. Atoms of the noble gases have a full set of electrons in their outer level.

- Hydrogen is set off by itself in the periodic table. Its properties do not match the properties of any one group.

Using Key Terms

Complete each of the following sentences by choosing the correct term from the word bank.

noble gas	alkaline-earth metal
halogen	alkali metal

1. An atom of a(n) ___ has a full set of electrons in its outermost energy level.

2. An atom of a(n) ___ has one electron in its outermost energy level.

3. An atom of a(n) ___ tends to gain one electron when it combines with another atom.

4. An atom of a(n) ___ tends to lose two electrons when it combines with another atom.

Understanding Key Ideas

5. Which group contains elements whose atoms have six electrons in their outer level?
   - **a.** Group 2
   - **b.** Group 6
   - **c.** Group 16
   - **d.** Group 18

6. What are two properties of the alkali metals?

7. What causes the properties of elements in a group to be similar?

8. What are two properties of the halogens?

9. Why is hydrogen set apart from the other elements in the periodic table?

10. Which group contains elements whose atoms have three electrons in their outer level?

Interpreting Graphics

11. Look at the model of an atom below. Does the model represent a metal atom or a nonmetal atom? Explain your answer.

Critical Thinking

12. **Making Inferences** Why are neither the alkali metals nor the alkaline-earth metals found uncombined in nature?

13. **Making Comparisons** Compare the element hydrogen with the alkali metal sodium.

For a variety of links related to this chapter, go to www.scilinks.org

Topic: Alkali Metals; Halogens and Noble Gases

SciLinks code: HSM0043; HSM0711

Model-Making Lab

Create a Periodic Table

You probably have classification systems for many things in your life, such as your clothes, your books, and your CDs. One of the most important classification systems in science is the periodic table of the elements. In this lab, you will develop your own classification system for a collection of ordinary objects. You will analyze trends in your system and compare your system with the periodic table of the elements.

OBJECTIVES

Classify objects based on their properties.

Identify patterns and trends in data.

MATERIALS

- bag of objects
- balance, metric
- meterstick
- paper, graphing (2 sheets)
- paper, 3 × 3 cm squares (20)

Procedure

1 Your teacher will give you a bag of objects. Your bag is missing one item. Examine the items carefully. Describe the missing object in as many ways as you can. Be sure to include the reasons why you think the missing object has the characteristics you describe.

2 Lay the paper squares out on your desk or table so that you have a grid of five rows of four squares each.

3 Arrange your objects on the grid in a logical order. (You must decide what order is logical!) You should end up with one blank square for the missing object.

4 Record a description of the basis for your arrangement.

5 Measure the mass (g) and diameter (mm) of each object, and record your results in the appropriate square. Each square (except the empty one) should have one object and two written measurements on it.

6 Examine your pattern again. Does the order in which your objects are arranged still make sense? Explain.

7 Rearrange the squares and their objects if necessary to improve your arrangement. Record a description of the basis for the new arrangement.

8 Working across the rows, number the squares 1 to 20. When you get to the end of a row, continue numbering in the first square of the next row.

9 Copy your grid. In each square, be sure to list the type of object and label all measurements with appropriate units.

Analyze the Results

1 **Constructing Graphs** Make a graph of mass (*y*-axis) versus object number (*x*-axis). Label each axis, and title the graph.

2 **Constructing Graphs** Now make a graph of diameter (*y*-axis) versus object number (*x*-axis).

Draw Conclusions

3 **Analyzing Graphs** Discuss each graph with your classmates. Try to identify any important features of the graph. For example, does the graph form a line or a curve? Is there anything unusual about the graph? What do these features tell you? Record your answers.

4 **Evaluating Models** How is your arrangement of objects similar to the periodic table of the elements found in this textbook? How is your arrangement different from that periodic table?

5 **Making Predictions** Look again at your prediction about the missing object. Do you think your prediction is still accurate? Try to improve your description by estimating the mass and diameter of the missing object. Record your estimates.

6 **Evaluating Methods** Mendeleev created a periodic table of elements and predicted characteristics of missing elements. How is your experiment similar to Mendeleev's work?

Chapter Review

USING KEY TERMS

Complete each of the following sentences by choosing the correct term from the word bank.

group   period
alkali metals   halogens
alkaline-earth metals noble gases

1 Elements in the same vertical column on the periodic table belong to the same ___.

2 Elements in the same horizontal row on the periodic table belong to the same ___.

3 The most reactive metals are ___.

4 Elements that are unreactive are called ___.

UNDERSTANDING KEY IDEAS

Multiple Choice

5 Mendeleev's periodic table was useful because it

 a. showed the elements arranged by atomic number.

 b. had no empty spaces.

 c. showed the atomic number of the elements.

 d. allowed for the prediction of the properties of missing elements.

6 Most nonmetals are

 a. shiny.

 b. poor conductors of electric current.

 c. flattened when hit with a hammer.

 d. solids at room temperature.

7 Which of the following items is NOT found on the periodic table?

 a. the atomic number of each element

 b. the name of each element

 c. the date that each element was discovered

 d. the atomic mass of each element

8 Which of the following statements about the periodic table is false?

 a. There are more metals than nonmetals on the periodic table.

 b. Atoms of elements in the same group have the same number of electrons in their outer level.

 c. The elements at the far left of the periodic table are nonmetals.

 d. Elements are arranged by increasing atomic number.

9 Which of the following statements about alkali metals is true?

 a. Alkali metals are generally found in their uncombined form.

 b. Alkali metals are Group 1 elements.

 c. Alkali metals should be stored underwater.

 d. Alkali metals are unreactive.

10 Which of the following statements about elements is true?

 a. Every element occurs naturally.

 b. All elements are found in their uncombined form in nature.

 c. Each element has a unique atomic number.

 d. All of the elements exist in approximately equal quantities.

Short Answer

11 How is Moseley's basis for arranging the elements different from Mendeleev's?

12 How is the periodic table like a calendar?

Math Skills

Examine the chart of the percentages of elements in the Earth's crust below. Then, answer the questions that follow.

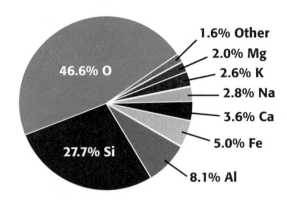

1.6% Other
2.0% Mg
2.6% K
2.8% Na
3.6% Ca
5.0% Fe
8.1% Al
27.7% Si
46.6% O

13 Excluding the "Other" category, what percentage of the Earth's crust are alkali metals?

14 Excluding the "Other" category, what percentage of the Earth's crust are alkaline-earth metals?

CRITICAL THINKING

15 **Concept Mapping** Use the following terms to create a concept map: *periodic table, elements, groups, periods, metals, nonmetals,* and *metalloids.*

16 **Forming Hypotheses** Why was Mendeleev unable to make any predictions about the noble gas elements?

17 **Identifying Relationships** When an element that has 115 protons in its nucleus is synthesized, will it be a metal, a nonmetal, or a metalloid? Explain your answer.

18 **Applying Concepts** Your classmate offers to give you a piece of sodium that he found on a hiking trip. What is your response? Explain.

19 **Applying Concepts** Identify each element described below.

a. This metal is very reactive, has properties similar to those of magnesium, and is in the same period as bromine.

b. This nonmetal is in the same group as lead.

INTERPRETING GRAPHICS

20 Study the diagram below to determine the pattern of the images. Predict the missing image, and draw it. Identify which properties are periodic and which properties are shared within a group.

READING

Read each of the passages below. Then, answer the questions that follow each passage.

Passage 1 Napoleon III (1808–1873) ruled as emperor of France from 1852 to 1870. Napoleon III was the nephew of the famous French military leader and emperor Napoleon I. Early in his reign, Napoleon III was an <u>authoritarian</u> ruler. France's economy did well under his dictatorial rule, so the French rebuilt cities and built railways. During the 1850s and 1860s, Napoleon III used aluminum dinnerware because aluminum was more valuable than gold. Despite his wealth and French economic prosperity, Napoleon III lost public support and popularity. So, in 1860, he began a series of reforms that allowed more individual freedoms in France.

1. What is the meaning of the word *authoritarian* in the passage?

  A controlling people's thoughts and actions

  B writing books and stories

  C being an expert on a subject

  D being very wealthy

2. Which of the following statements best describes why Napoleon III probably changed the way he ruled France?

  F He was getting old.

  G He was unpopular and had lost public support.

  H He had built as many railroads as he could.

  I He used aluminum dinnerware.

3. According to the passage, in what year did Napoleon III die?

  A 1808

  B 1873

  C 1860

  D 1852

Passage 2 Named after architect Buckminster Fuller, buckyballs resemble the geodesic domes that are characteristic of the architect's work. Excitement over buckyballs began in 1985, when scientists projected light from a laser onto a piece of graphite. In the soot that remained, researchers found a completely new kind of molecule! Buckyballs are also found in the soot from a candle flame. Some scientists claim to have detected buckyballs in space. In fact, one suggestion is that buckyballs are at the center of the condensing clouds of gas, dust, and debris that form galaxies.

1. Which of the following statements correctly describes buckyballs?

  A They are a kind of dome-shaped building.

  B They are shot from lasers.

  C They were unknown before 1985.

  D They are named for the scientist who discovered them.

2. Based on the passage, which of the following statements is an opinion?

  F Buckyballs might be in the clouds that form galaxies.

  G Buckyballs are named after an architect.

  H Scientists found buckyballs in soot.

  I Buckyballs are a kind of molecule.

3. According to the passage, why were scientists excited?

  A Buckyballs were found in space.

  B An architect created a building that resembled a molecule.

  C Buckyballs were found to be in condensing clouds of gas that form galaxies.

  D A new kind of molecule was found.

Use the image of the periodic table below to answer the questions that follow.

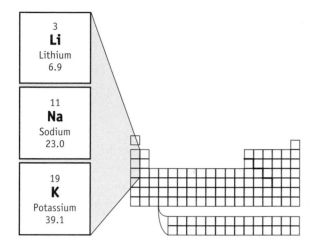

1. Which of the following statements is correct for the elements shown?

   A Lithium has the greatest atomic number.

   B Sodium has the least atomic mass.

   C Atomic number decreases as you move down the column.

   D Atomic mass increases as you move down the column.

2. Which of the following statements best describes the outer electrons in atoms of the elements shown?

   F The atoms of each element have 1 outer-level electron.

   G Lithium atoms have 3 outer-level electrons, sodium atoms have 11, and potassium atoms have 19.

   H Lithium atoms have 7 outer-level electrons, sodium atoms have 23, and potassium atoms have 39.

   I The atoms of each element have 11 outer-level electrons.

3. The elements featured in the image belong to which of the following groups?

   A noble gases

   B alkaline-earth metals

   C halogens

   D alkali metals

Read each question below, and choose the best answer.

1. Elvira's house is 7.3 km from her school. What is this distance expressed in meters?

   A 0.73 m

   B 73 m

   C 730 m

   D 7,300 m

2. A chemical company is preparing a shipment of 10 g each of four elements. Each element must be shipped in its own container that is completely filled with the element. Which container will be the largest?

Element	Density (g/cm³)	Mass (g)
Aluminum	2.702	10
Arsenic	5.727	10
Germanium	5.350	10
Silicon	2.420	10

   F the container of aluminum

   G the container of arsenic

   H the container of germanium

   I the container of silicon

3. Arjay has samples of several common elements. Each element has a unique atomic mass (expressed in amu). Which of the following lists shows the atomic masses in order from least to greatest?

   A 63.55, 58.69, 55.85, 58.93

   B 63.55, 58.93, 58.69, 55.85

   C 55.85, 58.69, 58.93, 63.55

   D 55.85, 63.55, 58.69, 58.93

Standardized Test Preparation

Science in Action

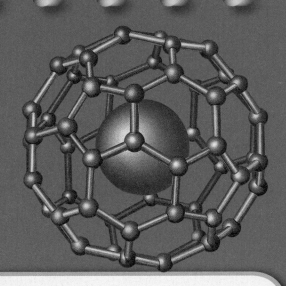

Weird Science

Buckyballs

In 1985, scientists found a completely new kind of molecule! This carbon molecule has 60 carbon atoms linked together in a shape similar to that of a soccer ball. This molecule is called a buckyball. Buckyballs have also been found in the soot from candle flames. And some scientists claim to have detected buckyballs in space. Chemists have been trying to identify the molecules' properties. One property is that a buckyball can act like a cage and hold smaller substances, such as individual atoms. Buckyballs are both slippery and strong. Scientists are exploring their use in tough plastics and cutting tools.

Language Arts ACTIVITY

WRITING SKILL Imagine that you are trapped within a buckyball. Write a one-page short story describing your experience. Describe the windows in your molecular prison.

Science, Technology, and Society

The Science of Fireworks

Explosive and dazzling, a fireworks display is both a science and an art. More than 1,000 years ago, the Chinese made black powder, or gunpowder. The powder was used to set off firecrackers and primitive missiles. The shells of fireworks contain several different chemicals. Black powder at the bottom of the shell launches the shell into the sky. A second layer of black powder ignites the rest of the chemicals and causes an explosion that lights up the sky! Colors can be created by mixing chemicals such as strontium (for red), magnesium (for white), or copper (for blue) with the gunpowder.

Math ACTIVITY

Fireworks can cost between $200 and $2,000 each. If a show uses 20 fireworks that cost $200 each, 12 fireworks that cost $500 each, and 10 fireworks that cost $1,200 each, what is the total cost for the fireworks?

Glenn T. Seaborg

Making Elements When you look at the periodic table, you can thank Dr. Glenn Theodore Seaborg and his colleagues for many of the actinide elements. While working at the University of California at Berkeley, Seaborg and his team added a number of elements to the periodic table. His work in identifying properties of plutonium led to his working on the top-secret Manhattan Project at the University of Chicago. He was outspoken about the beneficial uses of atomic energy and, at the same time, opposed the production and use of nuclear weapons.

Seaborg's revision of the layout of the periodic table—the actinide concept—is the most significant since Mendeleev's original design. For his scientific achievements, Dr. Seaborg was awarded the 1951 Nobel Prize in Chemistry jointly with his colleague, Dr. Edwin M. McMillan. Element 106, which Seaborg neither discovered nor created, was named seaborgium in his honor. This was the first time an element had been named after a living person.

Social Studies ACTIVITY

WRITING SKILL Write a newspaper editorial to express an opinion for or against the Manhattan Project. Be sure to include information to support your view.

go.hrw.com

To learn more about these Science in Action topics, visit **go.hrw.com** and type in the keyword **HP5PRTF.**

Current Science

Check out Current Science® articles related to this chapter by visiting go.hrw.com. Just type in the keyword **HP5CS12.**

Skills Practice Lab

Volumania!

You have learned how to measure the volume of a solid object that has square or rectangular sides. But there are lots of objects in the world that have irregular shapes. In this lab activity, you'll learn some ways to find the volume of objects that have irregular shapes.

Part A: Finding the Volume of Small Objects

Procedure

1 Fill a graduated cylinder half full with water. Read and record the volume of the water. Be sure to look at the surface of the water at eye level and to read the volume at the bottom of the meniscus, as shown below.

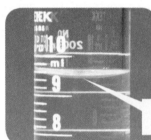

Read volume here

2 Carefully slide one of the objects into the tilted graduated cylinder, as shown below.

3 Read the new volume, and record it.

4 Subtract the old volume from the new volume. The resulting amount is equal to the volume of the solid object.

5 Use the same method to find the volume of the other objects. Record your results.

Analyze the Results

1 What changes do you have to make to the volumes you determine in order to express them correctly?

2 Do the heaviest objects always have the largest volumes? Why or why not?

MATERIALS

Part A

- graduated cylinder
- water
- various small objects supplied by your teacher

Part B

- bottle, plastic (or similar container), 2L, bottom half
- funnel
- graduated cylinder
- pan, aluminum pie
- paper towels
- water

SAFETY

Part B: Finding the Volume of Your Hand

Procedure

1. Completely fill the container with water. Put the container in the center of the pie pan. Be sure not to spill any of the water into the pie pan.

2. Make a fist, and put your hand into the container up to your wrist.

3. Remove your hand, and let the excess water drip into the container, not the pie pan. Dry your hand with a paper towel.

4. Use the funnel to pour the overflow water into the graduated cylinder. Measure the volume. This measurement is the volume of your hand. Record the volume. (Remember to use the correct unit of volume for a solid object.)

5. Repeat this procedure with your other hand.

Analyze the Results

1. Was the volume the same for both of your hands? If not, were you surprised? What might account for a person's hands having different volumes?

2. Would it have made a difference if you had placed your open hand into the container instead of your fist? Explain your reasoning.

3. Compare the volume of your right hand with the volume of your classmates' right hands. Create a class graph of right-hand volumes. What is the average right-hand volume for your class?

Applying Your Data

Design an experiment to determine the volume of a person's body. In your plans, be sure to include the materials needed for the experiment and the procedures that must be followed. Include a sketch that shows how your materials and methods would be used in this experiment.

Using an encyclopedia, the Internet, or other reference materials, find out how the volumes of very large samples of matter—such as an entire planet—are determined.

Skills Practice Lab

Determining Density

The density of an object is its mass divided by its volume. But how does the density of a small amount of a substance relate to the density of a larger amount of the same substance? In this lab, you will calculate the density of one marble and of a group of marbles. Then, you will confirm the relationship between the mass and volume of a substance.

MATERIALS

- balance, metric
- graduated cylinder, 100 mL
- marbles, glass (8–10)
- paper, graph
- paper towels
- water

SAFETY

Procedure

① Copy the table below. Include one row for each marble.

Mass of marble (g)	Total mass of marbles (g)	Total volume (mL)	Volume of marbles (mL) (total volume minus 50.0 mL)	Density of marbles (g/mL) (total mass divided by volume)
		DO NOT WRITE IN BOOK		

② Fill the graduated cylinder with 50 mL of water. If you put in too much water, twist one of the paper towels, and use it to absorb excess water.

③ Measure the mass of a marble as accurately as you can (to at least .01 g). Record the mass in the table.

④ Carefully drop the marble in the tilted cylinder, and measure the total volume. Record the volume in the third column.

⑤ Measure and record the mass of another marble. Add the masses of the marbles together, and record this value in the second column of the table.

⑥ Carefully drop the second marble in the graduated cylinder. Complete the row of information in the table.

⑦ Repeat steps 5 and 6. Add one marble at a time. Stop when you run out of marbles, the water no longer completely covers the marbles, or the graduated cylinder is full.

Analyze the Results

① Examine the data in your table. As the number of marbles increases, what happens to the total mass of the marbles? What happens to the volume of the marbles? What happens to the density of the marbles?

② Graph the total mass of the marbles (*y*-axis) versus the volume of the marbles (*x*-axis). Is the graph a straight line?

Draw Conclusions

③ Does the density of a substance depend on the amount of substance present? Explain how your results support your answer.

Applying Your Data

Calculate the slope of the graph. How does the slope compare with the values in the column entitled "Density of marbles"? Explain.

Skills Practice Lab

Layering Liquids

You have learned that liquids form layers according to the densities of the liquids. In this lab, you'll discover whether it matters in which order you add the liquids.

MATERIALS

- beaker (or other small, clear container)
- funnel (3)
- graduated cylinder, 10 mL (3)
- liquid A
- liquid B
- liquid C

SAFETY

Ask a Question

1 Does the order in which you add liquids of different densities to a container affect the order of the layers formed by those liquids?

Form a Hypothesis

2 Write a possible answer to the question above.

Test the Hypothesis

3 Using the graduated cylinders, add 10 mL of each liquid to the clear container. Remember to read the volume at the bottom of the meniscus, as shown below. Record the order in which you added the liquids.

4 Observe the liquids in the container. Sketch what you see. Be sure to label the layers and the colors.

5 Add 10 mL more of liquid C. Observe what happens, and record your observations.

6 Add 20 mL more of liquid A. Observe what happens, and record your observations.

4 Find out in what order your classmates added the liquids to the container. Compare your results with those of a classmate who added the liquids in a different order. Were your results different? Explain why or why not.

Draw Conclusions

5 Based on your results, evaluate your hypothesis from step 2.

Analyze the Results

1 Which of the liquids has the greatest density? Which has the least density? How can you tell?

2 Did the layers change position when you added more of liquid C? Explain your answer.

3 Did the layers change position when you added more of liquid A? Explain your answer.

Skills Practice Lab

Full of Hot Air!

Why do hot-air balloons float gracefully above Earth, but balloons you blow up fall to the ground? The answer has to do with the density of the air inside the balloon. *Density* is mass per unit volume, and volume is affected by changes in temperature. In this experiment, you will investigate the relationship between the temperature of a gas and its volume. Then, you will be able to determine how the temperature of a gas affects its density.

MATERIALS

- balloon
- beaker, 250 mL
- gloves, heat-resistant
- hot plate
- ice water
- pan, aluminum (2)
- ruler, metric
- water

SAFETY

Ask a Question

1 How does an increase or decrease in temperature affect the volume of a balloon?

Form a Hypothesis

2 Write a hypothesis that answers the question above.

Test the Hypothesis

3 Fill an aluminum pan with water about 4 cm to 5 cm deep. Put the pan on the hot plate, and turn the hot plate on.

4 Fill the other pan 4 cm to 5 cm deep with ice water.

5 Blow up a balloon inside the 500 mL beaker, as shown. The balloon should fill the beaker but should not extend outside the beaker. Tie the balloon at its opening.

6 Place the beaker and balloon in the ice water. Observe what happens. Record your observations.

7 Remove the balloon and beaker from the ice water. Observe the balloon for several minutes. Record any changes.

8 Put on heat-resistant gloves. When the hot water begins to boil, put the beaker and balloon in the hot water. Observe the balloon for several minutes, and record your observations.

9 Turn off the hot plate. When the water has cooled, carefully pour it into a sink.

Analyze the Results

1 Summarize your observations of the balloon. Relate your observations to Charles's law.

2 Was your hypothesis from step 2 supported? If not, revise your hypothesis.

Draw Conclusions

3 Based on your observations, how is the density of a gas affected by an increase or decrease in temperature?

Skills Practice Lab

Can Crusher

Condensation can occur when gas particles come near the surface of a liquid. The gas particles slow down because they are attracted to the liquid. This reduction in speed causes the gas particles to condense into a liquid. In this lab, you'll see that particles that have condensed into a liquid don't take up as much space and therefore don't exert as much pressure as they did in the gaseous state.

MATERIALS

- beaker, 1 L
- can, aluminum (2)
- gloves, heat-resistant
- hot plate
- tongs
- water

SAFETY

Procedure

❶ Fill the beaker with room-temperature water.

❷ Place just enough water in an aluminum can to slightly cover the bottom.

❸ Put on heat-resistant gloves. Place the aluminum can on a hot plate turned to the highest temperature setting.

❹ Heat the can until the water is boiling. Steam should be rising vigorously from the top of the can.

❺ Using tongs, quickly pick up the can, and place the top 2 cm of the can upside down in the 1 L beaker filled with water.

❻ Describe your observations.

Analyze the Results

❶ The can was crushed because the atmospheric pressure outside the can became greater than the pressure inside the can. Explain what happened inside the can to cause the difference in pressure.

Draw Conclusions

❷ Inside every popcorn kernel is a small amount of water. When you make popcorn, the water inside the kernels is heated until it becomes steam. Explain how the popping of the kernels is the opposite of what you saw in this lab. Be sure to address the effects of pressure in your explanation.

Applying Your Data

Try the experiment again, but use ice water instead of room-temperature water. Explain your results in terms of the effects of temperature.

Skills Practice Lab

A Sugar Cube Race!

If you drop a sugar cube into a glass of water, how long will it take to dissolve? What can you do to speed up the rate at which it dissolves? Should you change something about the water, the sugar cube, or the process? In other words, what variable should you change? Before reading further, make a list of variables that could be changed in this situation. Record your list.

MATERIALS

- beakers or other clear containers (2)
- clock or stopwatch
- graduated cylinder
- sugar cubes (2)
- water
- other materials approved by your teacher

SAFETY

Ask a Question

1. Write a question you can test about factors that affect the rate sugar dissolves.

Form a Hypothesis

2. Choose one variable to test. Record your choice, and predict how changing your variable will affect the rate of dissolving.

Test the Hypothesis

3. Pour 150 mL of water into one of the beakers. Add one sugar cube, and use the stopwatch to measure how long it takes for the sugar cube to dissolve. You must not disturb the sugar cube in any way! Record this time.

4. Be sure to get your teacher's approval before you begin. You may need additional equipment.

5. Prepare your materials to test the variable you have picked. When you are ready, start your procedure for speeding up the rate at which the sugar cube dissolves. Use the stopwatch to measure the time. Record this time.

Analyze the Results

1. Compare your results with the prediction you made in step 2. Was your prediction correct? Why or why not?

Draw Conclusions

2. Why was it necessary to observe the sugar cube dissolving on its own before you tested the variable?

3. Do you think changing more than one variable would speed up the rate of dissolving even more? Explain your reasoning.

4. Discuss your results with a group that tested a different variable. Which variable had a greater effect on the rate of dissolving?

Skills Practice Lab

Making Butter

A colloid is an interesting substance. It has properties of both solutions and suspensions. Colloidal particles are not heavy enough to settle out, so they remain evenly dispersed throughout the mixture. In this activity, you will make butter—a very familiar colloid—and observe the characteristics that classify butter as a colloid.

MATERIALS

- clock or stopwatch
- container with lid, small, clear
- heavy cream
- marble

SAFETY

Procedure

1 Place a marble inside the container, and fill the container with heavy cream. Put the lid tightly on the container.

2 Take turns shaking the container vigorously and constantly for 10 min. Record the time when you begin shaking. Every minute, stop shaking the container, and hold it up to the light. Record your observations.

3 Continue shaking the container, taking turns if necessary. When you see, hear, or feel any changes inside the container, note the time and change.

4 After 10 min of shaking, you should have a lump of "butter" surrounded by liquid inside the container. Describe both the butter and the liquid in detail.

5 Let the container sit for about 10 min. Observe the butter and liquid again, and record your observations.

Analyze the Results

1 When you noticed the change inside the container, what did you think was happening at that point?

2 Based on your observations, explain why butter is classified as a colloid.

3 What kind of mixture is the liquid that is left behind? Explain.

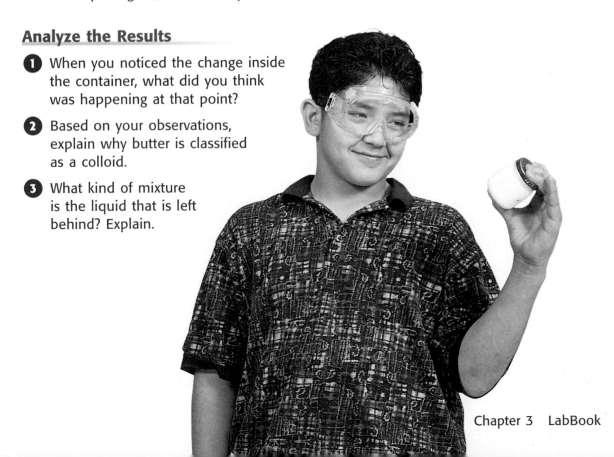

Model-Making Lab

Unpolluting Water

In many cities, the water supply comes from a river, lake, or reservoir. This water may include several mixtures, including suspensions (with suspended dirt, oil, or living organisms) and solutions (with dissolved chemicals). To make the water safe to drink, your city's water supplier must remove impurities. In this lab, you will model the procedures used in real water treatment plants.

MATERIALS

- beaker, 250 mL (4)
- charcoal, activated, washed
- cup, plastic-foam, 8 oz (2)
- graduated cylinder
- nail, small
- paper, filter (2 pieces)
- rubber band
- ruler, metric
- sand, fine, washed
- scissors
- spoon, plastic (2)
- water, "polluted"

SAFETY

Part A: Untreated Water

Procedure

1. Measure 100 mL of "polluted" water into a graduated cylinder. Be sure to shake the bottle of water before you pour so your sample will include all the impurities.

2. Pour the contents of the graduated cylinder into one of the beakers.

3. Copy the table below, and record your observations of the water in the "Before treatment" row.

Observations						
	Color	Clearness	Odor	Any layers?	Any solids?	Water volume
Before treatment						
After oil separation						
After sand filtration						
After charcoal						

DO NOT WRITE IN BOOK

Part B: Settling In

If a suspension is left standing, the suspended particles will settle to the top or bottom. You should see a layer of oil at the top.

Procedure

1. Separate the oil by carefully pouring the oil into another beaker. You can use a plastic spoon to get the last bit of oil from the water. Record your observations.

Part C: Filtration

Cloudy water can be a sign of small particles still in suspension. These particles can usually be removed by filtering. Water treatment plants use sand and gravel as filters.

Procedure

1 Make a filter as follows:

    a. Use the nail to poke 5 to 10 small holes in the bottom of one of the cups.

    b. Cut a circle of filter paper to fit inside the bottom of the cup. (This filter will keep the sand in the cup.)

    c. Fill the cup to 2 cm below the rim with wet sand. Pack the sand tightly.

    d. Set the cup inside an empty beaker.

2 Pour the polluted water on top of the sand, and let the water filter through. Do not pour any of the settled mud onto the sand. (Dispose of the mud as instructed by your teacher.) In your table, record your observations of the water collected in the beaker.

Part D: Separating Solutions

Something that has been dissolved in a solvent cannot be separated using filters. Water treatment plants use activated charcoal to absorb many dissolved chemicals.

Procedure

1 Place activated charcoal about 3 cm deep in the unused cup. Pour the water collected from the sand filtration into the cup, and stir with a spoon for 1 min.

2 Place a piece of filter paper over the top of the cup, and fasten it in place with a rubber band. With the paper securely in place, pour the water through the filter paper and back into a clean beaker. Record your observations in your table.

Analyze the Results

1 Is your unpolluted water safe to drink? Why or why not?

2 When you treat a sample of water, do you get out exactly the same amount of water that you put in? Explain your answer.

3 Some groups may still have cloudy water when they finish. Explain a possible cause for this.

Contents

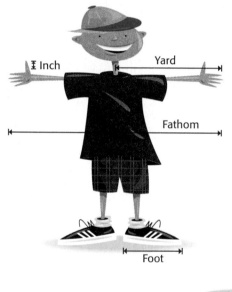

✓ *Reading Check* Answers

Chapter 1   The Properties of Matter
Section 1
Page 5: liters (L) and milliliters (mL)

Page 6: You could measure the volume of an apple by submerging the apple in a container of water and measuring the volume of the water that the apple displaces.

Page 8: kilograms (kg), grams (g), and milligrams (mg)

Section 2
Page 10: Some physical properties are color, shape, odor, weight, volume, texture, state, and density.

Page 12: If the object's density is less than the water's density, the object will float.

Page 15: A physical change is a change that occurs to a substance or object that does not change the identity of the substance.

Section 3
Page 16: Reactivity describes the ability of two or more substances to combine and form one or more new substances.

Page 18: Chemical changes occur when one or more substances are changed into entirely new substances that have different properties. A chemical property of a substance determines whether a chemical change will occur.

Chapter 2   States of Matter
Section 1
Page 33: The particles in a crystalline solid are arranged in a repeating pattern of rows that forms an orderly, three-dimensional arrangement.

Page 34: Viscosity is a liquid's resistance to flow.

Section 2
Page 37: There are more particles of gas in the basketball than there are in the beach ball. More particles hit the inside surface of the basketball, which causes increased force.

Page 38: Charles's law states that the volume of a gas in a closed container changes as the temperature of the gas changes. If the temperature increases, the volume increases. If the temperature decreases, the volume decreases.

Section 3
Page 40: A change of state is the change of a substance from one physical form to another.

Page 42: Evaporation is the change of a substance from a liquid to a gas.

Page 44: As a substance changes state, its temperature remains constant until the change of state is complete.

Chapter 3   Elements, Compounds, and Mixtures
Section 1
Page 56: An element is a pure substance because it contains only one type of particle.

Page 58: Metals are shiny, conduct heat energy, and conduct electric current.

Section 2
Page 61: Three physical properties used to identify compounds are melting point, density, and color.

Page 62: Compounds can be broken down into elements or simpler compounds.

Section 3
Page 64: Substances in a mixture keep their identities because no chemical change takes place when a mixture is made.

Page 67: An alloy is a solid solution of metal or nonmetal dissolved in another metal.

Page 69: As temperature increases, the solubility of a gas decreases.

Page 70: The particles of a suspension can be separated by passing the suspension through a filter.

Chapter 4   Introduction to Atoms
Section 1
Page 83: Dalton thought that elements are made of single atoms because elements always combine in specific proportions to form compounds.

Page 85: Rutherford could tell where the positively charged particles went because they hit a special coating that glowed where it was hit.

Page 86: Rutherford changed Thomson's model of the atom by proposing that the nucleus is a tiny, dense, positively charged area surrounded by electrons.

Section 2
Page 89: Protons and neutrons can be found in the nucleus.

Page 90: An atom becomes a positively charged ion when it loses an electron.

Page 92: Differences between isotopes are important when a certain isotope is radioactive.

Page 94: The four basic forces are the gravitational force, electromagnetic force, strong force, and weak force.

Chapter 5   The Periodic Table

Section 1

Page 106: Mendeleev had arranged elements based on increasing atomic mass.

Page 107: atomic number

Page 110: Most metals are solid at room temperature, ductile, malleable, and shiny. In addition, they are good conductors of electric current and thermal energy.

Page 112: Elements in a group often have similar chemical and physical properties.

Section 2

Page 115: It is easier for atoms of alkali metals to lose their outer electron than for atoms of transition metals to lose their outer electrons. Therefore, alkali metals are more reactive than transition metals.

Page 116: Yes, lanthanides and actinides are transition metals.

Page 117: silicon and germanium

Page 118: nitrogen and oxygen

Page 120: Atoms of noble gases have a full set of electrons in their outer level.

Appendix

Study Skills

FoldNote Instructions

Have you ever tried to study for a test or quiz but didn't know where to start? Or have you read a chapter and found that you can remember only a few ideas? Well, FoldNotes are a fun and exciting way to help you learn and remember the ideas you encounter as you learn science!

FoldNotes are tools that you can use to organize concepts. By focusing on a few main concepts, FoldNotes help you learn and remember how the concepts fit together. They can help you see the "big picture." Below you will find instructions for building 10 different FoldNotes.

Pyramid

1. Place a sheet of paper in front of you. Fold the lower left-hand corner of the paper diagonally to the opposite edge of the paper.

2. Cut off the tab of paper created by the fold (at the top).

3. Open the paper so that it is a square. Fold the lower right-hand corner of the paper diagonally to the opposite corner to form a triangle.

4. Open the paper. The creases of the two folds will have created an X.

5. Using scissors, cut along one of the creases. Start from any corner, and stop at the center point to create two flaps. Use tape or glue to attach one of the flaps on top of the other flap.

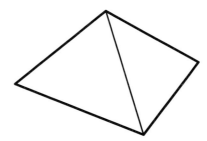

Double Door

1. Fold a sheet of paper in half from the top to the bottom. Then, unfold the paper.

2. Fold the top and bottom edges of the paper to the crease.

Booklet

1. Fold a sheet of paper in half from left to right. Then, unfold the paper.

2. Fold the sheet of paper in half again from the top to the bottom. Then, unfold the paper.

3. Refold the sheet of paper in half from left to right.

4. Fold the top and bottom edges to the center crease.

5. Completely unfold the paper.

6. Refold the paper from top to bottom.

7. Using scissors, cut a slit along the center crease of the sheet from the folded edge to the creases made in step 4. Do not cut the entire sheet in half.

8. Fold the sheet of paper in half from left to right. While holding the bottom and top edges of the paper, push the bottom and top edges together so that the center collapses at the center slit. Fold the four flaps to form a four-page book.

Layered Book

1. Lay one sheet of paper on top of another sheet. Slide the top sheet up so that 2 cm of the bottom sheet is showing.

2. Hold the two sheets together, fold down the top of the two sheets so that you see four 2 cm tabs along the bottom.

3. Using a stapler, staple the top of the FoldNote.

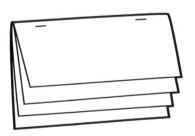

Key-Term Fold

1. Fold a sheet of lined notebook paper in half from left to right.

2. Using scissors, cut along every third line from the right edge of the paper to the center fold to make tabs.

Four-Corner Fold

1. Fold a sheet of paper in half from left to right. Then, unfold the paper.

2. Fold each side of the paper to the crease in the center of the paper.

3. Fold the paper in half from the top to the bottom. Then, unfold the paper.

4. Using scissors, cut the top flap creases made in step 3 to form four flaps.

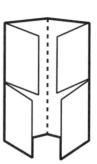

Three-Panel Flip Chart

1. Fold a piece of paper in half from the top to the bottom.

2. Fold the paper in thirds from side to side. Then, unfold the paper so that you can see the three sections.

3. From the top of the paper, cut along each of the vertical fold lines to the fold in the middle of the paper. You will now have three flaps.

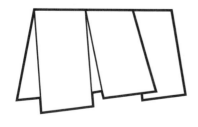

Table Fold

1. Fold a piece of paper in half from the top to the bottom. Then, fold the paper in half again.

2. Fold the paper in thirds from side to side.

3. Unfold the paper completely. Carefully trace the fold lines by using a pen or pencil.

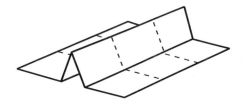

Two-Panel Flip Chart

1. Fold a piece of paper in half from the top to the bottom.

2. Fold the paper in half from side to side. Then, unfold the paper so that you can see the two sections.

3. From the top of the paper, cut along the vertical fold line to the fold in the middle of the paper. You will now have two flaps.

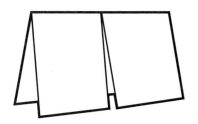

Tri-Fold

1. Fold a piece a paper in thirds from the top to the bottom.

2. Unfold the paper so that you can see the three sections. Then, turn the paper sideways so that the three sections form vertical columns.

3. Trace the fold lines by using a pen or pencil. Label the columns "Know," "Want," and "Learn."

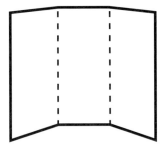

Appendix

Graphic Organizer Instructions

Have you ever wished that you could "draw out" the many concepts you learn in your science class? Sometimes, being able to *see* how concepts are related really helps you remember what you've learned. Graphic Organizers do just that! They give you a way to draw or map out concepts.

All you need to make a Graphic Organizer is a piece of paper and a pencil. Below you will find instructions for four different Graphic Organizers designed to help you organize the concepts you'll learn in this book.

Spider Map

1. Draw a diagram like the one shown. In the circle, write the main topic.

2. From the circle, draw legs to represent different categories of the main topic. You can have as many categories as you want.

3. From the category legs, draw horizontal lines. As you read the chapter, write details about each category on the horizontal lines.

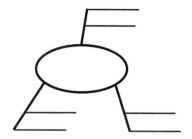

Comparison Table

1. Draw a chart like the one shown. Your chart can have as many columns and rows as you want.

2. In the top row, write the topics that you want to compare.

3. In the left column, write characteristics of the topics that you want to compare. As you read the chapter, fill in the characteristics for each topic in the appropriate boxes.

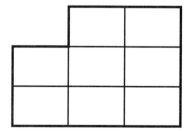

Chain-of-Events-Chart

1. Draw a box. In the box, write the first step of a process or the first event of a timeline.

2. Under the box, draw another box, and use an arrow to connect the two boxes. In the second box, write the next step of the process or the next event in the timeline.

3. Continue adding boxes until the process or timeline is finished.

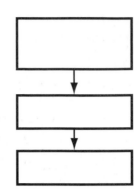

Concept Map

1. Draw a circle in the center of a piece of paper. Write the main idea of the chapter in the center of the circle.

2. From the circle, draw other circles. In those circles, write characteristics of the main idea. Draw arrows from the center circle to the circles that contain the characteristics.

3. From each circle that contains a characteristic, draw other circles. In those circles, write specific details about the characteristic. Draw arrows from each circle that contains a characteristic to the circles that contain specific details. You may draw as many circles as you want.

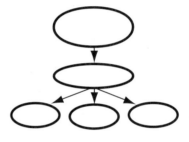

SI Measurement

The International System of Units, or SI, is the standard system of measurement used by many scientists. Using the same standards of measurement makes it easier for scientists to communicate with one another.

SI works by combining prefixes and base units. Each base unit can be used with different prefixes to define smaller and larger quantities. The table below lists common SI prefixes.

SI Prefixes

Prefix	Symbol	Factor	Example
kilo-	k	1,000	kilogram, 1 kg = 1,000 g
hecto-	h	100	hectoliter, 1 hL = 100 L
deka-	da	10	dekameter, 1 dam = 10 m
		1	meter, liter, gram
deci-	d	0.1	decigram, 1 dg = 0.1 g
centi-	c	0.01	centimeter, 1 cm = 0.01 m
milli-	m	0.001	milliliter, 1 mL = 0.001 L
micro-	μ	0.000 001	micrometer, 1 μm = 0.000 001 m

SI Conversion Table

SI units	From SI to English	From English to SI
Length		
kilometer (km) = 1,000 m	1 km = 0.621 mi	1 mi = 1.609 km
meter (m) = 100 cm	1 m = 3.281 ft	1 ft = 0.305 m
centimeter (cm) = 0.01 m	1 cm = 0.394 in.	1 in. = 2.540 cm
millimeter (mm) = 0.001 m	1 mm = 0.039 in.	
micrometer (μm) = 0.000 001 m		
nanometer (nm) = 0.000 000 001 m		
Area		
square kilometer (km^2) = 100 hectares	1 km^2 = 0.386 mi^2	1 mi^2 = 2.590 km^2
hectare (ha) = 10,000 m^2	1 ha = 2.471 acres	1 acre = 0.405 ha
square meter (m^2) = 10,000 cm^2	1 m^2 = 10.764 ft^2	1 ft^2 = 0.093 m^2
square centimeter (cm^2) = 100 mm^2	1 cm^2 = 0.155 $in.^2$	1 $in.^2$ = 6.452 cm^2
Volume		
liter (L) = 1,000 mL = 1 dm^3	1 L = 1.057 fl qt	1 fl qt = 0.946 L
milliliter (mL) = 0.001 L = 1 cm^3	1 mL = 0.034 fl oz	1 fl oz = 29.574 mL
microliter (μL) = 0.000 001 L		
Mass		*Equivalent weight at Earth's surface
kilogram (kg) = 1,000 g	1 kg = 2.205 lb*	1 lb* = 0.454 kg
gram (g) = 1,000 mg	1 g = 0.035 oz*	1 oz* = 28.350 g
milligram (mg) = 0.001 g		
microgram (μg) = 0.000 001 g		

Temperature Scales

Temperature can be expressed by using three different scales: Fahrenheit, Celsius, and Kelvin. The SI unit for temperature is the kelvin (K).

Although 0 K is much colder than 0°C, a change of 1 K is equal to a change of 1°C.

Three Temperature Scales

	Fahrenheit	Celsius	Kelvin
Water boils	212°	100°	373
Body temperature	98.6°	37°	310
Room temperature	68°	20°	293
Water freezes	32°	0°	273

Temperature Conversions Table

To convert	Use this equation:	Example
Celsius to Fahrenheit °C → °F	$°F = \left(\dfrac{9}{5} \times °C\right) + 32$	Convert 45°C to °F. $°F = \left(\dfrac{9}{5} \times 45°C\right) + 32 = 113°F$
Fahrenheit to Celsius °F → °C	$°C = \dfrac{5}{9} \times (°F - 32)$	Convert 68°F to °C. $°C = \dfrac{5}{9} \times (68°F - 32) = 20°C$
Celsius to Kelvin °C → K	$K = °C + 273$	Convert 45°C to K. $K = 45°C + 273 = 318\ K$
Kelvin to Celsius K → °C	$°C = K - 273$	Convert 32 K to °C. $°C = 32K - 273 = -241°C$

Measuring Skills

Using a Graduated Cylinder

When using a graduated cylinder to measure volume, keep the following procedures in mind:

1 Place the cylinder on a flat, level surface before measuring liquid.

2 Move your head so that your eye is level with the surface of the liquid.

3 Read the mark closest to the liquid level. On glass graduated cylinders, read the mark closest to the center of the curve in the liquid's surface.

Using a Meterstick or Metric Ruler

When using a meterstick or metric ruler to measure length, keep the following procedures in mind:

1 Place the ruler firmly against the object that you are measuring.

2 Align one edge of the object exactly with the 0 end of the ruler.

3 Look at the other edge of the object to see which of the marks on the ruler is closest to that edge. (Note: Each small slash between the centimeters represents a millimeter, which is one-tenth of a centimeter.)

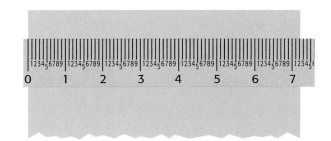

Using a Triple-Beam Balance

When using a triple-beam balance to measure mass, keep the following procedures in mind:

1 Make sure the balance is on a level surface.

2 Place all of the countermasses at 0. Adjust the balancing knob until the pointer rests at 0.

3 Place the object you wish to measure on the pan. **Caution:** Do not place hot objects or chemicals directly on the balance pan.

4 Move the largest countermass along the beam to the right until it is at the last notch that does not tip the balance. Follow the same procedure with the next-largest countermass. Then, move the smallest countermass until the pointer rests at 0.

5 Add the readings from the three beams together to determine the mass of the object.

6 When determining the mass of crystals or powders, first find the mass of a piece of filter paper. Then, add the crystals or powder to the paper, and remeasure. The actual mass of the crystals or powder is the total mass minus the mass of the paper. When finding the mass of liquids, first find the mass of the empty container. Then, find the combined mass of the liquid and container. The mass of the liquid is the total mass minus the mass of the container.

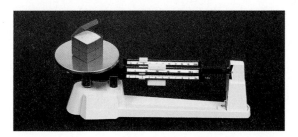

Scientific Methods

The ways in which scientists answer questions and solve problems are called **scientific methods.** The same steps are often used by scientists as they look for answers. However, there is more than one way to use these steps. Scientists may use all of the steps or just some of the steps during an investigation. They may even repeat some of the steps. The goal of using scientific methods is to come up with reliable answers and solutions.

Six Steps of Scientific Methods

 **1 Ask a Question** Good questions come from careful **observations.** You make observations by using your senses to gather information. Sometimes, you may use instruments, such as microscopes and telescopes, to extend the range of your senses. As you observe the natural world, you will discover that you have many more questions than answers. These questions drive investigations.

Questions beginning with *what, why, how,* and *when* are important in focusing an investigation. Here is an example of a question that could lead to an investigation.

Question: How does acid rain affect plant growth?

 **2 Form a Hypothesis** After you ask a question, you need to form a **hypothesis.** A hypothesis is a clear statement of what you expect the answer to your question to be. Your hypothesis will represent your best "educated guess" based on what you have observed and what you already know. A good hypothesis is testable. Otherwise, the investigation can go no further. Here is a hypothesis based on the question, "How does acid rain affect plant growth?"

Hypothesis: Acid rain slows plant growth.

The hypothesis can lead to predictions. A prediction is what you think the outcome of your experiment or data collection will be. Predictions are usually stated in an if-then format. Here is a sample prediction for the hypothesis that acid rain slows plant growth.

Prediction: If a plant is watered with only acid rain (which has a pH of 4), then the plant will grow at half its normal rate.

 **3 Test the Hypothesis** After you have formed a hypothesis and made a prediction, your hypothesis should be tested. One way to test a hypothesis is with a controlled experiment. A **controlled experiment** tests only one factor at a time. In an experiment to test the effect of acid rain on plant growth, the **control group** would be watered with normal rain water. The **experimental group** would be watered with acid rain. All of the plants should receive the same amount of sunlight and water each day. The air temperature should be the same for all groups. However, the acidity of the water will be a variable. In fact, any factor that is different from one group to another is a **variable.** If your hypothesis is correct, then the acidity of the water and plant growth are *dependant variables.* The amount a plant grows is dependent on the acidity of the water. However, the amount of water each plant receives and the amount of sunlight each plant receives are *independent variables.* Either of these factors could change without affecting the other factor.

Sometimes, the nature of an investigation makes a controlled experiment impossible. For example, the Earth's core is surrounded by thousands of meters of rock. Under such circumstances, a hypothesis may be tested by making detailed observations.

 **4 Analyze the Results** After you have completed your experiments, made your observations, and collected your data, you must analyze all the information you have gathered. Tables and graphs are often used in this step to organize the data.

 **Draw Conclusions**

After analyzing your data, you can determine if your results support your hypothesis. If your hypothesis is supported, you (or others) might want to repeat the observations or experiments to verify your results. If your hypothesis is not supported by the data, you may have to check your procedure for errors. You may even have to reject your hypothesis and make a new one. If you cannot draw a conclusion from your results, you may have to try the investigation again or carry out further observations or experiments.

 **Communicate Results**

After any scientific investigation, you should report your results. By preparing a written or oral report, you let others know what you have learned. They may repeat your investigation to see if they get the same results. Your report may even lead to another question and then to another investigation.

Scientific Methods in Action

Scientific methods contain loops in which several steps may be repeated over and over again. In some cases, certain steps are unnecessary. Thus, there is not a "straight line" of steps. For example, sometimes scientists find that testing one hypothesis raises new questions and new hypotheses to be tested. And sometimes, testing the hypothesis leads directly to a conclusion. Furthermore, the steps in scientific methods are not always used in the same order. Follow the steps in the diagram, and see how many different directions scientific methods can take you.

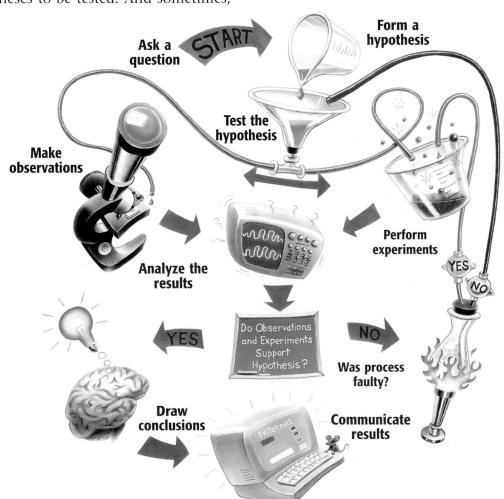

Periodic Table of the Elements

Each square on the table includes an element's name, chemical symbol, atomic number, and atomic mass.

The color of the chemical symbol indicates the physical state at room temperature. Carbon is a solid.

6	—— Atomic number
C	—— Chemical symbol
Carbon	—— Element name
12.0	—— Atomic mass

The background color indicates the type of element. Carbon is a nonmetal.

Background
- Metals
- Metalloids
- Nonmetals

Chemical symbol
- Solid
- Liquid
- Gas

Period 1

| 1 |
| **H** |
| Hydrogen |
| 1.0 |

	Group 1	Group 2
Period 2	3 **Li** Lithium 6.9	4 **Be** Beryllium 9.0
Period 3	11 **Na** Sodium 23.0	12 **Mg** Magnesium 24.3

	Group 1	Group 2	Group 3	Group 4	Group 5	Group 6	Group 7	Group 8	Group 9
Period 4	19 **K** Potassium 39.1	20 **Ca** Calcium 40.1	21 **Sc** Scandium 45.0	22 **Ti** Titanium 47.9	23 **V** Vanadium 50.9	24 **Cr** Chromium 52.0	25 **Mn** Manganese 54.9	26 **Fe** Iron 55.8	27 **Co** Cobalt 58.9
Period 5	37 **Rb** Rubidium 85.5	38 **Sr** Strontium 87.6	39 **Y** Yttrium 88.9	40 **Zr** Zirconium 91.2	41 **Nb** Niobium 92.9	42 **Mo** Molybdenum 95.9	43 **Tc** Technetium (98)	44 **Ru** Ruthenium 101.1	45 **Rh** Rhodium 102.9
Period 6	55 **Cs** Cesium 132.9	56 **Ba** Barium 137.3	57 **La** Lanthanum 138.9	72 **Hf** Hafnium 178.5	73 **Ta** Tantalum 180.9	74 **W** Tungsten 183.8	75 **Re** Rhenium 186.2	76 **Os** Osmium 190.2	77 **Ir** Iridium 192.2
Period 7	87 **Fr** Francium (223)	88 **Ra** Radium (226)	89 **Ac** Actinium (227)	104 **Rf** Rutherfordium (261)	105 **Db** Dubnium (262)	106 **Sg** Seaborgium (266)	107 **Bh** Bohrium (264)	108 **Hs** Hassium (277)	109 **Mt** Meitnerium (268)

A row of elements is called a *period*.

A column of elements is called a *group* or *family*.

Values in parentheses are the mass numbers of those radioactive elements' most stable or most common isotopes.

These elements are placed below the table to allow the table to be narrower.

Lanthanides	58 **Ce** Cerium 140.1	59 **Pr** Praseodymium 140.9	60 **Nd** Neodymium 144.2	61 **Pm** Promethium (145)	62 **Sm** Samarium 150.4
Actinides	90 **Th** Thorium 232.0	91 **Pa** Protactinium 231.0	92 **U** Uranium 238.0	93 **Np** Neptunium (237)	94 **Pu** Plutonium (244)

Topic: **Periodic Table**
Go To: **go.hrw.com**
Keyword: **HN0 PERIODIC**
Visit the HRW Web site for
updates on the periodic table.

Group 18

2
He
Helium
4.0

This zigzag line reminds you where the metals, nonmetals, and metalloids are.

Group 13	Group 14	Group 15	Group 16	Group 17
5	6	7	8	9	10
B	**C**	**N**	**O**	**F**	**Ne**
Boron	Carbon	Nitrogen	Oxygen	Fluorine	Neon
10.8	12.0	14.0	16.0	19.0	20.2
13	14	15	16	17	18
Al	**Si**	**P**	**S**	**Cl**	**Ar**
Aluminum	Silicon	Phosphorus	Sulfur	Chlorine	Argon
27.0	28.1	31.0	32.1	35.5	39.9

Group 10	Group 11	Group 12					
28	29	30	31	32	33	34	35	36
Ni	**Cu**	**Zn**	**Ga**	**Ge**	**As**	**Se**	**Br**	**Kr**
Nickel	Copper	Zinc	Gallium	Germanium	Arsenic	Selenium	Bromine	Krypton
58.7	63.5	65.4	69.7	72.6	74.9	79.0	79.9	83.8
46	47	48	49	50	51	52	53	54
Pd	**Ag**	**Cd**	**In**	**Sn**	**Sb**	**Te**	**I**	**Xe**
Palladium	Silver	Cadmium	Indium	Tin	Antimony	Tellurium	Iodine	Xenon
106.4	107.9	112.4	114.8	118.7	121.8	127.6	126.9	131.3
78	79	80	81	82	83	84	85	86
Pt	**Au**	**Hg**	**Tl**	**Pb**	**Bi**	**Po**	**At**	**Rn**
Platinum	Gold	Mercury	Thallium	Lead	Bismuth	Polonium	Astatine	Radon
195.1	197.0	200.6	204.4	207.2	209.0	(209)	(210)	(222)
110	111	112	113	114	115			
Ds	**Uuu**	**Uub**	**Uut**	**Uuq**	**Uup**			
Darmstadtium	Unununium	Ununbium	Ununtrium	Ununquadium	Ununpentium			
(281)	(272)	(285)	(284)	(289)	(288)			

The discovery of elements 113, 114, and 115 has been reported but not confirmed.

The names and three-letter symbols of elements are temporary. They are based on the atomic numbers of the elements. Official names and symbols will be approved by an international committee of scientists.

63	64	65	66	67	68	69	70	71
Eu	**Gd**	**Tb**	**Dy**	**Ho**	**Er**	**Tm**	**Yb**	**Lu**
Europium	Gadolinium	Terbium	Dysprosium	Holmium	Erbium	Thulium	Ytterbium	Lutetium
152.0	157.2	158.9	162.5	164.9	167.3	168.9	173.0	175.0
95	96	97	98	99	100	101	102	103
Am	**Cm**	**Bk**	**Cf**	**Es**	**Fm**	**Md**	**No**	**Lr**
Americium	Curium	Berkelium	Californium	Einsteinium	Fermium	Mendelevium	Nobelium	Lawrencium
(243)	(247)	(247)	(251)	(252)	(257)	(258)	(259)	(262)

Appendix

Making Charts and Graphs

Pie Charts

A pie chart shows how each group of data relates to all of the data. Each part of the circle forming the chart represents a category of the data. The entire circle represents all of the data. For example, a biologist studying a hardwood forest in Wisconsin found that there were five different types of trees. The data table at right summarizes the biologist's findings.

Wisconsin Hardwood Trees	
Type of tree	Number found
Oak	600
Maple	750
Beech	300
Birch	1,200
Hickory	150
Total	3,000

How to Make a Pie Chart

1 To make a pie chart of these data, first find the percentage of each type of tree. Divide the number of trees of each type by the total number of trees, and multiply by 100.

$$\frac{600 \text{ oak}}{3,000 \text{ trees}} \times 100 = 20\%$$

$$\frac{750 \text{ maple}}{3,000 \text{ trees}} \times 100 = 25\%$$

$$\frac{300 \text{ beech}}{3,000 \text{ trees}} \times 100 = 10\%$$

$$\frac{1,200 \text{ birch}}{3,000 \text{ trees}} \times 100 = 40\%$$

$$\frac{150 \text{ hickory}}{3,000 \text{ trees}} \times 100 = 5\%$$

2 Now, determine the size of the wedges that make up the pie chart. Multiply each percentage by 360°. Remember that a circle contains 360°.

$20\% \times 360° = 72°$ $25\% \times 360° = 90°$
$10\% \times 360° = 36°$ $40\% \times 360° = 144°$
$5\% \times 360° = 18°$

3 Check that the sum of the percentages is 100 and the sum of the degrees is 360.

$20\% + 25\% + 10\% + 40\% + 5\% = 100\%$
$72° + 90° + 36° + 144° + 18° = 360°$

4 Use a compass to draw a circle and mark the center of the circle.

5 Then, use a protractor to draw angles of 72°, 90°, 36°, 144°, and 18° in the circle.

6 Finally, label each part of the chart, and choose an appropriate title.

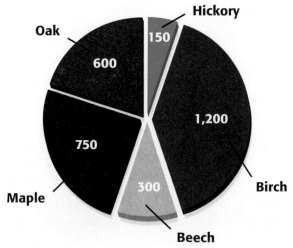

A Community of Wisconsin Hardwood Trees

Oak 600 · Hickory 150 · Maple 750 · Beech 300 · Birch 1,200

Line Graphs

Line graphs are most often used to demonstrate continuous change. For example, Mr. Smith's students analyzed the population records for their hometown, Appleton, between 1900 and 2000. Examine the data at right.

Because the year and the population change, they are the *variables*. The population is determined by, or dependent on, the year. Therefore, the population is called the **dependent variable**, and the year is called the **independent variable**. Each set of data is called a **data pair.** To prepare a line graph, you must first organize data pairs into a table like the one at right.

Population of Appleton, 1900–2000	
Year	Population
1900	1,800
1920	2,500
1940	3,200
1960	3,900
1980	4,600
2000	5,300

How to Make a Line Graph

1 Place the independent variable along the horizontal (*x*) axis. Place the dependent variable along the vertical (*y*) axis.

2 Label the *x*-axis "Year" and the *y*-axis "Population." Look at your largest and smallest values for the population. For the *y*-axis, determine a scale that will provide enough space to show these values. You must use the same scale for the entire length of the axis. Next, find an appropriate scale for the *x*-axis.

3 Choose reasonable starting points for each axis.

4 Plot the data pairs as accurately as possible.

5 Choose a title that accurately represents the data.

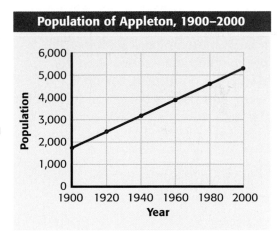

Population of Appleton, 1900–2000

How to Determine Slope

Slope is the ratio of the change in the *y*-value to the change in the *x*-value, or "rise over run."

1 Choose two points on the line graph. For example, the population of Appleton in 2000 was 5,300 people. Therefore, you can define point *a* as (2000, 5,300). In 1900, the population was 1,800 people. You can define point *b* as (1900, 1,800).

2 Find the change in the *y*-value. (*y* at point *a*) − (*y* at point *b*) = 5,300 people − 1,800 people = 3,500 people

3 Find the change in the *x*-value. (*x* at point *a*) − (*x* at point *b*) = 2000 − 1900 = 100 years

4 Calculate the slope of the graph by dividing the change in *y* by the change in *x*.

$$slope = \frac{change\ in\ y}{change\ in\ x}$$

$$slope = \frac{3,500\ people}{100\ years}$$

$$slope = 35\ people\ per\ year$$

In this example, the population in Appleton increased by a fixed amount each year. The graph of these data is a straight line. Therefore, the relationship is **linear.** When the graph of a set of data is not a straight line, the relationship is **nonlinear.**

Using Algebra to Determine Slope

The equation in step 4 may also be arranged to be

$$y = kx$$

where y represents the change in the y-value, k represents the slope, and x represents the change in the x-value.

$$slope = \frac{change\ in\ y}{change\ in\ x}$$

$$k = \frac{y}{x}$$

$$k \times x = \frac{y \times x}{x}$$

$$kx = y$$

Bar Graphs

Bar graphs are used to demonstrate change that is not continuous. These graphs can be used to indicate trends when the data cover a long period of time. A meteorologist gathered the precipitation data shown here for Hartford, Connecticut, for April 1–15, 1996, and used a bar graph to represent the data.

Precipitation in Hartford, Connecticut April 1–15, 1996			
Date	Precipitation (cm)	Date	Precipitation (cm)
April 1	0.5	April 9	0.25
April 2	1.25	April 10	0.0
April 3	0.0	April 11	1.0
April 4	0.0	April 12	0.0
April 5	0.0	April 13	0.25
April 6	0.0	April 14	0.0
April 7	0.0	April 15	6.50
April 8	1.75		

How to Make a Bar Graph

1 Use an appropriate scale and a reasonable starting point for each axis.

2 Label the axes, and plot the data.

3 Choose a title that accurately represents the data.

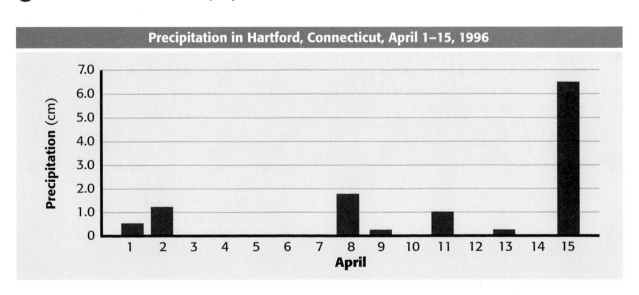

Math Refresher

Science requires an understanding of many math concepts. The following pages will help you review some important math skills.

Averages

An **average,** or **mean,** simplifies a set of numbers into a single number that *approximates* the value of the set.

Example: Find the average of the following set of numbers: 5, 4, 7, and 8.

Step 1: Find the sum.
$$5 + 4 + 7 + 8 = 24$$

Step 2: Divide the sum by the number of numbers in your set. Because there are four numbers in this example, divide the sum by 4.
$$\frac{24}{4} = 6$$

The average, or mean, is **6.**

Ratios

A **ratio** is a comparison between numbers, and it is usually written as a fraction.

Example: Find the ratio of thermometers to students if you have 36 thermometers and 48 students in your class.

Step 1: Make the ratio.
$$\frac{36 \text{ thermometers}}{48 \text{ students}}$$

Step 2: Reduce the fraction to its simplest form.
$$\frac{36}{48} = \frac{36 \div 12}{48 \div 12} = \frac{3}{4}$$

The ratio of thermometers to students is **3 to 4,** or $\frac{3}{4}$. The ratio may also be written in the form 3:4.

Proportions

A **proportion** is an equation that states that two ratios are equal.
$$\frac{3}{1} = \frac{12}{4}$$

To solve a proportion, first multiply across the equal sign. This is called *cross-multiplication.* If you know three of the quantities in a proportion, you can use cross-multiplication to find the fourth.

Example: Imagine that you are making a scale model of the solar system for your science project. The diameter of Jupiter is 11.2 times the diameter of the Earth. If you are using a plastic-foam ball that has a diameter of 2 cm to represent the Earth, what must the diameter of the ball representing Jupiter be?
$$\frac{11.2}{1} = \frac{x}{2 \text{ cm}}$$

Step 1: Cross-multiply.
$$\frac{11.2}{1} \diagdown\!\!\!\!\!\diagup \frac{x}{2}$$
$$11.2 \times 2 = x \times 1$$

Step 2: Multiply.
$$22.4 = x \times 1$$

Step 3: Isolate the variable by dividing both sides by 1.
$$x = \frac{22.4}{1}$$
$$x = 22.4 \text{ cm}$$

You will need to use a ball that has a diameter of **22.4** cm to represent Jupiter.

Appendix

Percentages

A **percentage** is a ratio of a given number to 100.

> **Example:** What is 85% of 40?

Step 1: Rewrite the percentage by moving the decimal point two places to the left.

$$0.\underset{\smile}{85}$$

Step 2: Multiply the decimal by the number that you are calculating the percentage of.

$$0.85 \times 40 = 34$$

85% of 40 is **34.**

Decimals

To **add** or **subtract decimals,** line up the digits vertically so that the decimal points line up. Then, add or subtract the columns from right to left. Carry or borrow numbers as necessary.

> **Example:** Add the following numbers: 3.1415 and 2.96.

Step 1: Line up the digits vertically so that the decimal points line up.

$$\begin{array}{r} 3.1415 \\ +\ 2.96 \\ \hline \end{array}$$

Step 2: Add the columns from right to left, and carry when necessary.

$$\begin{array}{r} {}^{1\ 1} \\ 3.1415 \\ +\ 2.96 \\ \hline 6.1015 \end{array}$$

The sum is **6.1015.**

Fractions

Numbers tell you how many; **fractions** tell you *how much of a whole.*

> **Example:** Your class has 24 plants. Your teacher instructs you to put 5 plants in a shady spot. What fraction of the plants in your class will you put in a shady spot?

Step 1: In the denominator, write the total number of parts in the whole.

$$\frac{?}{24}$$

Step 2: In the numerator, write the number of parts of the whole that are being considered.

$$\frac{5}{24}$$

So, $\frac{5}{24}$ of the plants will be in the shade.

Reducing Fractions

It is usually best to express a fraction in its simplest form. Expressing a fraction in its simplest form is called *reducing* a fraction.

> **Example:** Reduce the fraction $\frac{30}{45}$ to its simplest form.

Step 1: Find the largest whole number that will divide evenly into both the numerator and denominator. This number is called the *greatest common factor* (GCF).

Factors of the numerator 30:
    1, 2, 3, 5, 6, 10, **15,** 30

Factors of the denominator 45:
    1, 3, 5, 9, **15,** 45

Step 2: Divide both the numerator and the denominator by the GCF, which in this case is 15.

$$\frac{30}{45} = \frac{30 \div 15}{45 \div 15} = \frac{2}{3}$$

Thus, $\frac{30}{45}$ reduced to its simplest form is $\frac{2}{3}$.

Appendix

Adding and Subtracting Fractions

To **add** or **subtract fractions** that have the **same denominator,** simply add or subtract the numerators.

Examples:

$$\frac{3}{5} + \frac{1}{5} = ? \text{ and } \frac{3}{4} - \frac{1}{4} = ?$$

Step 1: Add or subtract the numerators.

$$\frac{3}{5} + \frac{1}{5} = \frac{4}{} \text{ and } \frac{3}{4} - \frac{1}{4} = \frac{2}{}$$

Step 2: Write the sum or difference over the denominator.

$$\frac{3}{5} + \frac{1}{5} = \frac{4}{5} \text{ and } \frac{3}{4} - \frac{1}{4} = \frac{2}{4}$$

Step 3: If necessary, reduce the fraction to its simplest form.

$$\frac{4}{5} \text{ cannot be reduced, and } \frac{2}{4} = \frac{1}{2}.$$

To **add** or **subtract fractions** that have **different denominators,** first find the least common denominator (LCD).

Examples:

$$\frac{1}{2} + \frac{1}{6} = ? \text{ and } \frac{3}{4} - \frac{2}{3} = ?$$

Step 1: Write the equivalent fractions that have a common denominator.

$$\frac{3}{6} + \frac{1}{6} = ? \text{ and } \frac{9}{12} - \frac{8}{12} = ?$$

Step 2: Add or subtract the fractions.

$$\frac{3}{6} + \frac{1}{6} = \frac{4}{6} \text{ and } \frac{9}{12} - \frac{8}{12} = \frac{1}{12}$$

Step 3: If necessary, reduce the fraction to its simplest form.

The fraction $\frac{4}{6} = \frac{2}{3}$, and $\frac{1}{12}$ cannot be reduced.

Multiplying Fractions

To **multiply fractions,** multiply the numerators and the denominators together, and then reduce the fraction to its simplest form.

Example:

$$\frac{5}{9} \times \frac{7}{10} = ?$$

Step 1: Multiply the numerators and denominators.

$$\frac{5}{9} \times \frac{7}{10} = \frac{5 \times 7}{9 \times 10} = \frac{35}{90}$$

Step 2: Reduce the fraction.

$$\frac{35}{90} = \frac{35 \div 5}{90 \div 5} = \frac{7}{18}$$

Dividing Fractions

To **divide fractions,** first rewrite the divisor (the number you divide by) upside down. This number is called the *reciprocal* of the divisor. Then multiply and reduce if necessary.

Example:

$$\frac{5}{8} \div \frac{3}{2} = ?$$

Step 1: Rewrite the divisor as its reciprocal.

$$\frac{3}{2} \rightarrow \frac{2}{3}$$

Step 2: Multiply the fractions.

$$\frac{5}{8} \times \frac{2}{3} = \frac{5 \times 2}{8 \times 3} = \frac{10}{24}$$

Step 3: Reduce the fraction.

$$\frac{10}{24} = \frac{10 \div 2}{24 \div 2} = \frac{5}{12}$$

Appendix

Scientific Notation

Scientific notation is a short way of representing very large and very small numbers without writing all of the place-holding zeros.

Example: Write 653,000,000 in scientific notation.

Step 1: Write the number without the place-holding zeros.

653

Step 2: Place the decimal point after the first digit.

6.53

Step 3: Find the exponent by counting the number of places that you moved the decimal point.

6.53000000

The decimal point was moved eight places to the left. Therefore, the exponent of 10 is positive 8. If you had moved the decimal point to the right, the exponent would be negative.

Step 4: Write the number in scientific notation.

6.53×10^8

Area

Area is the number of square units needed to cover the surface of an object.

Formulas:

$area\ of\ a\ square = side \times side$

$area\ of\ a\ rectangle = length \times width$

$area\ of\ a\ triangle = \frac{1}{2} \times base \times height$

Examples: Find the areas.

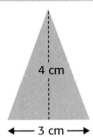

Triangle

$area = \frac{1}{2} \times base \times height$

$area = \frac{1}{2} \times 3\ cm \times 4\ cm$

$area = \textbf{6 cm}^2$

4 cm

3 cm

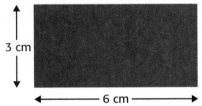

3 cm

6 cm

Rectangle

$area = length \times width$

$area = 6\ cm \times 3\ cm$

$area = \textbf{18 cm}^2$

3 cm

3 cm

Square

$area = side \times side$

$area = 3\ cm \times 3\ cm$

$area = \textbf{9 cm}^2$

Volume

Volume is the amount of space that something occupies.

Formulas:

$volume\ of\ a\ cube =$
$side \times side \times side$

$volume\ of\ a\ prism =$
$area\ of\ base \times height$

Examples:

Find the volume of the solids.

Cube

$volume = side \times side \times side$

$volume = 4\ cm \times 4\ cm \times 4\ cm$

$volume = \textbf{64 cm}^3$

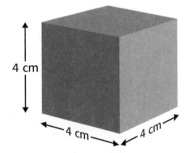

4 cm

4 cm

4 cm

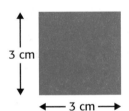

4 cm

3 cm

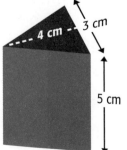

5 cm

Prism

$volume = area\ of\ base \times height$

$volume = (area\ of\ triangle) \times height$

$volume = (\frac{1}{2} \times 3\ cm \times 4\ cm) \times 5\ cm$

$volume = 6\ cm^2 \times 5\ cm$

$volume = \textbf{30 cm}^3$

Physical Science Laws and Principles

Law of Conservation of Mass

Mass cannot be created or destroyed during ordinary chemical or physical changes.

The total mass in a closed system is always the same no matter how many physical changes or chemical reactions occur.

Law of Conservation of Energy

Energy can be neither created nor destroyed.

The total amount of energy in a closed system is always the same. Energy can be changed from one form to another, but all of the different forms of energy in a system always add up to the same total amount of energy no matter how many energy conversions occur.

Law of Universal Gravitation

All objects in the universe attract each other by a force called *gravity*. The size of the force depends on the masses of the objects and the distance between the objects.

The first part of the law explains why lifting a bowling ball is much harder than lifting a marble. Because the bowling ball has a much larger mass than the marble does, the amount of gravity between the Earth and the bowling ball is greater than the amount of gravity between the Earth and the marble.

The second part of the law explains why a satellite can remain in orbit around the Earth. The satellite is carefully placed at a distance great enough to prevent the Earth's gravity from immediately pulling the satellite down but small enough to prevent the satellite from completely escaping the Earth's gravity and wandering off into space.

Newton's Laws of Motion

Newton's first law of motion states that an object at rest remains at rest and an object in motion remains in motion at constant speed and in a straight line unless acted on by an unbalanced force.

The first part of the law explains why a football will remain on a tee until it is kicked off or until a gust of wind blows it off.

The second part of the law explains why a bike rider will continue moving forward after the bike comes to an abrupt stop. Gravity and the friction of the sidewalk will eventually stop the rider.

Newton's second law of motion states that the acceleration of an object depends on the mass of the object and the amount of force applied.

The first part of the law explains why the acceleration of a 4 kg bowling ball will be greater than the acceleration of a 6 kg bowling ball if the same force is applied to both balls.

The second part of the law explains why the acceleration of a bowling ball will be larger if a larger force is applied to the bowling ball.

The relationship of acceleration (a) to mass (m) and force (F) can be expressed mathematically by the following equation:

$$acceleration = \frac{force}{mass}, \text{ or } a = \frac{F}{m}$$

This equation is often rearranged to the form

$$force = mass \times acceleration, \text{ or } F = m \times a$$

Newton's third law of motion states that whenever one object exerts a force on a second object, the second object exerts an equal and opposite force on the first.

This law explains that a runner is able to move forward because of the equal and opposite force that the ground exerts on the runner's foot after each step.

Law of Reflection

The law of reflection states that the angle of incidence is equal to the angle of reflection. This law explains why light reflects off a surface at the same angle that the light strikes the surface.

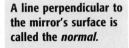

A line perpendicular to the mirror's surface is called the *normal*.

The beam of light reflected off the mirror is called the *reflected beam*.

The beam of light traveling toward the mirror is called the *incident beam*.

The angle between the incident beam and the normal is called the *angle of incidence*.

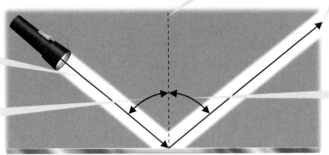

The angle between the reflected beam and the normal is called the *angle of reflection*.

Charles's Law

Charles's law states that for a fixed amount of gas at a constant pressure, the volume of the gas increases as the temperature of the gas increases. Likewise, the volume of the gas decreases as the temperature of the gas decreases.

If a basketball that was inflated indoors is left outside on a cold winter day, the air particles inside the ball will move more slowly. They will hit the sides of the basketball less often and with less force. The ball will get smaller as the volume of the air decreases.

Boyle's Law

Boyle's law states that for a fixed amount of gas at a constant temperature, the volume of a gas increases as the pressure of the gas decreases. Likewise, the volume of a gas decreases as its pressure increases.

If an inflated balloon is pulled down to the bottom of a swimming pool, the pressure of the water on the balloon increases. The pressure of the air particles inside the balloon must increase to match that of the water outside, so the volume of the air inside the balloon decreases.

Pascal's Principle

Pascal's principle states that a change in pressure at any point in an enclosed fluid will be transmitted equally to all parts of that fluid.

When a mechanic uses a hydraulic jack to raise an automobile off the ground, he or she increases the pressure on the fluid in the jack by pushing on the jack handle. The pressure is transmitted equally to all parts of the fluid-filled jacking system. As fluid presses the jack plate against the frame of the car, the car is lifed off the ground.

Archimedes' Principle

Archimedes' principle states that the buoyant force on an object in a fluid is equal to the weight of the volume of fluid that the object displaces.

A person floating in a swimming pool displaces 20 L of water. The weight of that volume of water is about 200 N. Therefore, the buoyant force on the person is 200 N.

Bernoulli's Principle

Bernoulli's principle states that as the speed of a moving fluid increases, the fluid's pressure decreases.

The lift on an airplane wing or on a Frisbee® can be explained in part by using Bernoulli's principle. Because of the shape of the Frisbee, the air moving over the top of the Frisbee must travel farther than the air below the Frisbee in the same amount of time. In other words, the air above the Frisbee is moving faster than the air below it. This faster-moving air above the Frisbee exerts less pressure than the slower-moving air below it does. The resulting increased pressure below exerts an upward force and pushes the Frisbee up.

Useful Equations

Average speed

$$average\ speed = \frac{total\ distance}{total\ time}$$

Example: A bicycle messenger traveled a distance of 136 km in 8 h. What was the messenger's average speed?

$$\frac{136\ km}{8\ h} = 17\ km/h$$

The messenger's average speed was **17 km/h.**

Average acceleration

$$\frac{average}{acceleration} = \frac{final\ velocity - starting\ velocity}{time\ it\ takes\ to\ change\ velocity}$$

Example: Calculate the average acceleration of an Olympic 100 m dash sprinter who reaches a velocity of 20 m/s south at the finish line. The race was in a straight line and lasted 10 s.

$$\frac{20\ m/s - 0\ m/s}{10s} = 2\ m/s/s$$

The sprinter's average acceleration is **2 m/s/s south.**

Net force

Forces in the Same Direction

When forces are in the same direction, add the forces together to determine the net force.

Example: Calculate the net force on a stalled car that is being pushed by two people. One person is pushing with a force of 13 N northwest, and the other person is pushing with a force of 8 N in the same direction.

$$13\ N + 8\ N = 21\ N$$

The net force is **21 N northwest.**

Forces in Opposite Directions

When forces are in opposite directions, subtract the smaller force from the larger force to determine the net force. The net force will be in the direction of the larger force.

Example: Calculate the net force on a rope that is being pulled on each end. One person is pulling on one end of the rope with a force of 12 N south. Another person is pulling on the opposite end of the rope with a force of 7 N north.

$$12\ N - 7\ N = 5\ N$$

The net force is **5 N south.**

Work

Work is done by exerting a force through a distance. Work has units of joules (J), which are equivalent to Newton-meters.

$$Work = F \times d$$

Example: Calculate the amount of work done by a man who lifts a 100 N toddler 1.5 m off the floor.

$Work = 100 \text{ N} \times 1.5 \text{ m} = 150 \text{ N•m} = 150 \text{ J}$

The man did **150 J** of work.

Power

Power is the rate at which work is done. Power is measured in watts (W), which are equivalent to joules per second.

$$P = \frac{Work}{t}$$

Example: Calculate the power of a weightlifter who raises a 300 N barbell 2.1 m off the floor in 1.25 s.

$Work = 300 \text{ N} \times 2.1 \text{ m} = 630 \text{ N•m} = 630 \text{ J}$

$$P = \frac{630 \text{ J}}{1.25 \text{ s}} = \frac{504 \text{ J}}{\text{s}} = 504 \text{ W}$$

The weightlifter has **504 W** of power.

Pressure

Pressure is the force exerted over a given area. The SI unit for pressure is the pascal (Pa).

$$pressure = \frac{force}{area}$$

Example: Calculate the pressure of the air in a soccer ball if the air exerts a force of 25,000 N over an area of 0.15 m^2.

$$pressure = \frac{25,000 \text{ N}}{0.15 \text{ m}^2} = \frac{167,000 \text{ N}}{\text{m}^2} = 167,000 \text{ Pa}$$

The pressure of the air inside the soccer ball is **167,000 Pa.**

Density

$$density = \frac{mass}{volume}$$

Example: Calculate the density of a sponge that has a mass of 10 g and a volume of 40 cm^3.

$$\frac{10 \text{ g}}{40 \text{ cm}^3} = \frac{0.25 \text{ g}}{\text{cm}^3}$$

The density of the sponge is $\frac{0.25 \text{ g}}{\text{cm}^3}$.

Concentration

$$concentration = \frac{mass \text{ } of \text{ } solute}{volume \text{ } of \text{ } solvent}$$

Example: Calculate the concentration of a solution in which 10 g of sugar is dissolved in 125 mL of water.

$$\frac{10 \text{ g of sugar}}{125 \text{ mL of water}} = \frac{0.08 \text{ g}}{\text{mL}}$$

The concentration of this solution is $\frac{0.08 \text{ g}}{\text{mL}}$.

Glossary

A

alkali metal (AL kuh LIE MET uhl) one of the elements of Group 1 of the periodic table (lithium, sodium, potassium, rubidium, cesium, and francium) (114)

alkaline-earth metal (AL kuh LIEN UHRTH MET uhl) one of the elements of Group 2 of the periodic table (beryllium, magnesium, calcium, strontium, barium, and radium) (115)

atom the smallest unit of an element that maintains the properties of that element (82)

atomic mass the mass of an atom expressed in atomic mass units (93)

atomic mass unit a unit of mass that describes the mass of an atom or molecule (89)

atomic number the number of protons in the nucleus of an atom; the atomic number is the same for all atoms of an element (91)

B

boiling the conversion of a liquid to a vapor when the vapor pressure of the liquid equals the atmospheric pressure (42)

Boyle's law the law that states that the volume of a gas is inversely proportional to the pressure of a gas when temperature is constant (38)

C

change of state the change of a substance from one physical state to another (40)

Charles's law the law that states that the volume of a gas is directly proportional to the temperature of a gas when pressure is constant (38)

chemical change a change that occurs when one or more substances change into entirely new substances with different properties (18)

chemical property a property of matter that describes a substance's ability to participate in chemical reactions (16)

colloid (KAHL OYD) a mixture consisting of tiny particles that are intermediate in size between those in solutions and those in suspensions and that are suspended in a liquid, solid, or gas (70)

compound a substance made up of atoms of two or more different elements joined by chemical bonds (60)

concentration the amount of a particular substance in a given quantity of a mixture, solution, or ore (68)

condensation the change of state from a gas to a liquid (43)

D

density the ratio of the mass of a substance to the volume of the substance (11)

E

electron a subatomic particle that has a negative charge (84)

electron cloud a region around the nucleus of an atom where electrons are likely to be found (87)

element a substance that cannot be separated or broken down into simpler substances by chemical means (56)

evaporation (ee vap uh RAY shuhn) the change of a substance from a liquid to a gas (42)

G

gas a form of matter that does not have a definite volume or shape (35)

group a vertical column of elements in the periodic table; elements in a group share chemical properties (112

H

halogen (HAL oh juhn) one of the elements of Group 17 of the periodic table (fluorine, chlorine, bromine, iodine, and astatine); halogens combine with most metals to form salts (119)

I

inertia (in UHR shuh) the tendency of an object to resist being moved or, if the object is moving, to resist a change in speed or direction until an outside force acts on the object (8)

isotope (IE suh TOHP) an atom that has the same number of protons (or the same atomic number) as other atoms of the same element do but that has a different number of neutrons (and thus a different atomic mass) (91)

L

liquid the state of matter that has a definite volume but not a definite shape (34)

M

mass a measure of the amount of matter in an object (7)

mass number the sum of the numbers of protons and neutrons in the nucleus of an atom (92)

matter anything that has mass and takes up space (4)

melting the change of state in which a solid becomes a liquid by adding heat (41)

meniscus (muh NIS kuhs) the curve at a liquid's surface by which one measures the volume of the liquid (5)

metal an element that is shiny and that conducts heat and electricity well (58)

metalloid elements that have properties of both metals and nonmetals (58)

mixture a combination of two or more substances that are not chemically combined (64)

N

neutron a subatomic particle that has no charge and that is found in the nucleus of an atom (89)

noble gas one of the elements of Group 18 of the periodic table (helium, neon, argon, krypton, xenon, and radon); noble gases are unreactive (120)

nonmetal an element that conducts heat and electricity poorly (58)

nucleus (NOO klee uhs) in physical science, an atom's central region, which is made up of protons and neutrons (86)

P

period in chemistry, a horizontal row of elements in the periodic table (112)

periodic describes something that occurs or repeats at regular intervals (107)

periodic law the law that states that the repeating chemical and physical properties of elements change periodically with the atomic numbers of the elements (107)

physical change a change of matter from one form to another without a change in chemical properties (14)

physical property a characteristic of a substance that does not involve a chemical change, such as density, color, or hardness (10)

pressure the amount of force exerted per unit area of a surface (37)

proton a subatomic particle that has a positive charge and that is found in the nucleus of an atom (89)

pure substance a sample of matter, either a single element or a single compound, that has definite chemical and physical properties (56)

S

solid the state of matter in which the volume and shape of a substance are fixed (33)

solubility the ability of one substance to dissolve in another at a given temperature and pressure (68)

solute in a solution, the substance that dissolves in the solvent (66)

solution a homogeneous mixture of two or more substances uniformly dispersed throughout a single phase (66)

solvent in a solution, the substance in which the solute dissolves (66)

states of matter the physical forms of matter, which include solid, liquid, and gas (32)

sublimation (SUHB luh MAY shuhn) the process in which a solid changes directly into a gas (44)

surface tension the force that acts on the surface of a liquid and that tends to minimize the area of the surface (34)

suspension a mixture in which particles of a material are more or less evenly dispersed throughout a liquid or gas (70)

T

temperature a measure of how hot (or cold) something is; specifically, a measure of the average kinetic energy of the particles in an object (36)

V

viscosity the resistance of a gas or liquid to flow (34)

volume a measure of the size of a body or region in three-dimensional space (4, 37)

W

weight a measure of the gravitational force exerted on an object; its value can change with the location of the object in the universe (7)

Glossary

Spanish Glossary

A

alkali metal/metal alcalino uno de los elementos del Grupo 1 de la tabla periódica (litio, sodio, potasio, rubidio, cesio y francio) (114)

alkaline-earth metal/metal alcalinotérreo uno de los elementos del Grupo 2 de la tabla periódica (berilio, magnesio, calcio, estroncio, bario y radio) (115)

atom/átomo la unidad más pequeña de un elemento que conserva las propiedades de ese elemento (82)

atomic mass/masa atómica la masa de un átomo, expresada en unidades de masa atómica (93)

atomic mass unit/unidad de masa atómica una unidad de masa que describe la masa de un átomo o una molécula (89)

atomic number/número atómico el número de protones en el núcleo de un átomo; el número atómico es el mismo para todos los átomos de un elemento (91)

B

boiling/ebullición la conversión de un líquido en vapor cuando la presión de vapor del líquido es igual a la presión atmosférica (42)

Boyle's law/ley de Boyle la ley que establece que el volumen de un gas es inversamente proporcional a su presión cuando la temperatura es constante (38)

C

change of state/cambio de estado el cambio de una substancia de un estado físico a otro (40)

Charles's law/ley de Charles la ley que establece que el volumen de un gas es directamente proporcional a su temperatura cuando la presión es constante (38)

chemical change/cambio químico un cambio que ocurre cuando una o más substancias se transforman en substancias totalmente nuevas con propiedades diferentes (18)

chemical property/propiedad química una propiedad de la materia que describe la capacidad de una substancia de participar en reacciones químicas (16)

colloid/coloide una mezcla formada por partículas diminutas que son de tamaño intermedio entre las partículas de las soluciones y las de las suspensiones y que se encuentran suspendidas en un líquido, sólido o gas (70)

compound/compuesto una substancia formada por átomos de dos o más elementos diferentes unidos por enlaces químicos (94)

compound machine/máquina compuesta una máquina hecha de más de una máquina simple (60)

concentration/concentración la cantidad de una cierta substancia en una cantidad determinada de mezcla, solución o mena (68)

condensation/condensación el cambio de estado de gas a líquido (43)

D

density/densidad la relación entre la masa de una substancia y su volumen (11)

E

electron/electrón una partícula subatómica que tiene carga negativa (84)

electron cloud/nube de electrones una región que rodea al núcleo de un átomo en la cual es probable encontrar a los electrones (87)

element/elemento una substancia que no se puede separar o descomponer en substancias más simples por medio de métodos químicos (56)

evaporation/evaporación el cambio de una substancia de líquido a gas (42)

G

gas/gas un estado de la materia que no tiene volumen ni forma definidos (35)

group/grupo una columna vertical de elementos de la tabla periódica; los elementos de un grupo comparten propiedades químicas (112)

H

halogen/halógeno uno de los elementos del Grupo 17 de la tabla periódica (flúor, cloro, bromo, yodo y ástato); los halógenos se combinan con la mayoría de los metales para formar sales (119)

I

inertia/inercia la tendencia de un objeto a no moverse o, si el objeto se está moviendo, la tendencia a resistir un cambio en su rapidez o dirección hasta que una fuerza externa actúe en el objeto (8)

isotope/isótopo un átomo que tiene el mismo número de protones (o el mismo número atómico) que otros átomos del mismo elemento, pero que tiene un número diferente de neutrones (y, por lo tanto, otra masa atómica) (91)

L

liquid/líquido el estado de la materia que tiene un volumen definido, pero no una forma definida (34)

M

mass/masa una medida de la cantidad de materia que tiene un objeto (7)

mass number/número de masa la suma de los números de protones y neutrones que hay en el núcleo de un átomo (92)

matter/materia cualquier cosa que tiene masa y ocupa un lugar en el espacio (4)

melting/fusión el cambio de estado en el que un sólido se convierte en líquido al añadirse calor (41)

meniscus/menisco la curva que se forma en la superficie de un líquido, la cual sirve para medir el volumen de un líquido (5)

metal/metal un elemento que es brillante y conduce bien el calor y la electricidad (58)

metalloid/metaloides elementos que tienen propiedades tanto de metales como de no metales (58)

mixture/mezcla una combinación de dos o más substancias que no están combinadas químicamente (64)

N

neutron/neutrón una partícula subatómica que no tiene carga y que se encuentra en el núcleo de un átomo (89)

uno de los elementos del Grupo 18 de la tabla periódica (helio, neón, argón, criptón, xenón y radón); los gases nobles son no reactivos (120)

nonmetal/no metal un elemento que es mal conductor del calor y la electricidad (58)

nucleus/núcleo en ciencias físicas, la región central de un átomo, la cual está constituida por protones y neutrones (86)

P

period/período en química, una hilera horizontal de elementos en la tabla periódica (112)

periodic/periódico término que describe algo que ocurre o que se repite a intervalos regulares (107)

periodic law/ley periódica la ley que establece que las propiedades químicas y físicas repetitivas de un elemento cambian periódicamente en función del número atómico de los elementos (107)

physical change/cambio físico un cambio de materia de una forma a otra sin que ocurra un cambio en sus propiedades químicas (14)

physical property/propiedad física una característica de una substancia que no implica un cambio químico, tal como la densidad, el color o la dureza (10)

pressure/presión la cantidad de fuerza ejercida en una superficie por unidad de área (37)

proton/protón una partícula subatómica que tiene una carga positiva y que se encuentra en el núcleo de un átomo (89)

pure substance/substancia pura una muestra de materia, ya sea un solo elemento o un solo compuesto, que tiene propiedades químicas y físicas definidas (56)

S

solid/sólido el estado de la materia en el cual el volumen y la forma de una sustancia están fijos (33)

solubility/solubilidad la capacidad de una substancia de disolverse en otra a una temperatura y una presión dadas (68)

solute/soluto en una solución, la sustancia que se disuelve en el solvente (66)

solution/solución una mezcla homogénea de dos o más sustancias dispersas de manera uniforme en una sola fase (66)

solvent/solvente en una solución, la sustancia en la que se disuelve el soluto (66)

states of matter/estados de la material las formas físicas de la materia, que son sólida, líquida y gaseosa (32)

sublimation/sublimación el proceso por medio del cual un sólido se transforma directamente en un gas (44)

surface tension/tensión superficial la fuerza que actúa en la superficie de un líquido y que tiende a minimizar el área de la superficie (34)

suspension/suspensión una mezcla en la que las partículas de un material se encuentran dispersas de manera más o menos uniforme a través de un líquido o de un gas (70)

T

temperature/temperatura una medida de qué tan caliente (o frío) está algo; específicamente, una medida de la energía cinética promedio de las partículas de un objeto (36)

V

viscosity/viscosidad la resistencia de un gas o un líquido a fluir (34)

volume/volumen una medida del tamaño de un cuerpo o región en un espacio de tres dimensiones (4, 37)

W

weight/peso una medida de la fuerza gravitacional ejercida sobre un objeto; su valor puede cambiar en función de la ubicación del objeto en el universo (7)

Spanish Glossary

Index

Boldface page numbers refer to illustrative material, such as figures, tables, margin elements, photographs, and illustrations.

Index

Index

Index

Index

Credits

Abbreviations used: (t) top, (c) center, (b) bottom, (l) left, (r) right, (bkgd) background

PHOTOGRAPHY

Front Cover Burke/Triolo Productions/Getty Images

Skills Practice Lab Teens Sam Dudgeon/HRW

Connection to Astronomy Corbis Images; **Connection to Biology** David M. Phillips/Visuals Unlimited; **Connection to Chemistry** Digital Image copyright © 2005 PhotoDisc; **Connection to Environment** Digital Image copyright © 2005 PhotoDisc; **Connection to Geology** Letraset Phototone; **Connection to Language Arts** Digital Image copyright © 2005 PhotoDisc; **Connection to Meteorology** Digital Image copyright © 2005 PhotoDisc; **Connection to Oceanography** © ICONOTEC; **Connection to Physics** Digital Image copyright © 2005 PhotoDisc

Table of Contents iv (cl), Richard Megna/Fundamental Photographs; iv (b), Victoria Smith/HRW; v (t), Sam Dudgeon/HRW; v (cl), Corbis Images; vi–vii, Victoria Smith/HRW; x (bl), Sam Dudgeon/HRW; xi (tl), John Langford/HRW; xi (b), Sam Dudgeon/HRW; xii (tl), Victoria Smith/HRW; xii (bl), Stephanie Morris/HRW; xii (br), Sam Dudgeon/HRW; xiii (tl), Patti Murray/Animals, Animals; xiii (tr), Jana Birchum/HRW; xiii (b), Peter Van Steen/HRW

Chapter One 2–3 (all), Mark Renders/Getty Images; 4 (b), Sam Dudgeon/HRW; 4 (bc), Digital Image copyright © 2005 PhotoDisc; 5 (cr), Sam Dudgeon/HRW; 6 (cl), Sam Dudgeon/HRW; 6 (cl), Victoria Smith/HRW; 7 (all), Sam Dudgeon/HRW; 8 (tl), John Langford/HRW; 8 (br), Corbis Images; 10 (b), Sam Dudgeon/HRW; 11 (tl), Victoria Smith/HRW; 11 (tr, tc, c), Sam Dudgeon/HRW; 11 (cl), Peter Van Steen/HRW; 11 (cr, bl), John Morrison/Morrison Photography; 12 (tl), Richard Megna/Fundamental Photographs; 12 (bl), Victoria Smith/HRW; 14 (tr), Lance Schriner/HRW; 14 (tl), John Langford/HRW; 15 (tr), Victoria Smith/HRW; 15 (inset), Sam Dudgeon/HRW; 16 (br), Rob Boudreau/Getty Images; 17 (cl, cr), Charlie Winters/HRW; 17 (tl, tr), Sam Dudgeon/HRW; 18 (c, cr), Morrison Photography; 18 (bl), Joseph Drivas/Getty Images; 18 (br), © SuperStock; 19 (all), Sam Dudgeon/HRW; 20 (all), Charlie Winters/HRW; 21 (tr), CORBIS Images/HRW; 22 (b), Sam Dudgeon/HRW; 24 (bc), Richard Megna/Fundamental Photographs; 25 (cr), Lance Schriner/HRW; 28 (tl), © David Young–Wolff/PhotoEdit; 29 (cr), Courtesy Mimi So; 29 (b), Steve Cole/PhotoDisc/PictureQuest

Chapter Two 30–31 (all), Teresa Nouri Rishel/Dale Chihuly Studio; 33 (bl), Digital Image copyright © 2005 PhotoDisc; 33 (br), Susumu Nishinaga/Science Photo Library/Photo Researchers, Inc.; 34 (tr), Victoria Smith/HRW; 34 (bl), © Dr Jeremy Burgess/Photo Researchers, Inc.; 35 (tr), Scott Van Osdol/HRW; 36 (br), AP Photo/Beth Keiser; 37 (bl), Corbis Images; 37 (br), Victoria Smith/HRW; 41 (bc), Scott Van Osdol/HRW; 41 (tr), Richard Megna/Fundamental Photographs; 43 (bl), Ed Reschke/Peter Arnold, Inc.; 44 (tl), Omni Photo Communications, Inc./Index Stock Imagery, Inc.; 46 (br), Victoria Smith/HRW; 47 (br), Sam Dudgeon/HRW; 48 (bc), Sam Dudgeon/HRW; 49 (bl), Charles D. Winters/Photo Researchers, Inc.; 52 (tr), CORBIS Images/HRW; 52 (tl), Scoones/SIPA Press; 53 (cr), Susanna Frohman/San Jose Mercury News/NewsCom; 53 (bl), Andrew Goldsworthy

Chapter Three 54–55 (all), Scott Van Osdol/HRW; 56 (br), Jonathan Blair/Woodfin Camp & Associates, Inc.; 56 (bl), Victoria Smith/HRW; 57 (br), Russ Lappa/Photo Researchers, Inc.; 57 (bl, bc), Charles D. Winters/Photo Researchers, Inc.; 58 (tl), © Zack Burris/Zack Burris, Inc.; 58 (tcl), Yann Arthus–Bertrand/CORBIS; 58 (tcr, tr), Walter Chandoha; 59 (lead), Victoria Smith/HRW; 59 (copper, tin, sulfur), Sam Dudgeon/HRW; 59 (neon), Runk/Shoenberger/Grant Heilman Photography Inc.; 59 (silicon), Joyce Photographics/Photo Researchers, Inc.; 59 (boron), Russ Lappa/Photo Researchers, Inc.; 59 (antimony), Charles D. Winters/Photo Researchers, Inc.; 59 (iodine), Larry Stepanowicz; 60 (bl), Runk/Shoenberger/Grant Heilman Photography Inc.; 61 (bl), Runk/Shoenberger/Grant Heilman Photography; 61 (bc), Richard Megna/Fundamental Photographs; 61 (br), Sam Dudgeon/HRW; 62 (tl), Richard Megna/Fundamental Photographs; 63 (tr), John Kaprielian/Photo Researchers, Inc.; 64 (br), Sam Dudgeon/HRW; 65 (tl), Charles D. Winters; 65 (cl), Sam Dudgeon/HRW; 65 (bc), Charles D. Winters/Photo Researchers, Inc.; 65 (bl), Klaus Guldbrandsen/Science Photo Library/Photo Researchers, Inc.; 65 (tr, cr, br), John Langford/HRW; 66 (tl), Sam Dudgeon/HRW; 67 (bl), Richard Haynes/HRW; 68 (tr), Sam Dudgeon/HRW; 69 (all), John Langford/HRW; 70 (bl), HRW; 70 (br), Lance Schriner/HRW; 71 (tr), Sam Dudgeon/HRW; 72 (bl), © Stuart Westmoreland/Getty Images; 73 (b), Sam Dudgeon/HRW; 74 (tr), Sam Dudgeon/HRW; 74 (tl), Walter Chandoha; 75 (tr), Sam Dudgeon/HRW; 78 (tl), Peter Van Steen/HRW; 79 (tr), Courtesy of Aundra Nix; 79 (cr), Astrid & Hans–Frieder Michler/SPL/Photo Researchers, Inc.

Chapter Four 80–81 (all), P. Loiez Cern/Science Photo Library/Photo Researchers, Inc.; 82 (bl), Victoria Smith/HRW; 83 (b), Corbis–Bettmann; 86 (br), John Zoiner; 86 (bc), Mavournea Hay/HRW; 88 (b), Sam Dudgeon/HRW; 93 (tr), Corbis Images; 95 (b), Sam Dudgeon/HRW; 96 (br), Victoria Smith/HRW; 97 (br), Sam Dudgeon/HRW; 98 (bl), Corbis–Bettmann; 99 (bl), Fermilab; 102 (tr), NASA; 102 (tl), Giraudon/Art Resource, NY; 103 (br), Fermi National Accelerator Laboratory/CORBIS; 103 (tr), Stephen Maclone

Chapter Five 104–105 (all), Gerard Perrone/Courtesy of Eric Ehlenberger; 107 (tr), Sam Dudgeon/HRW; 110 (all), Sam Dudgeon/HRW; 111 (tr), Sam Dudgeon/HRW; 111 (tc), Richard Megna/Fundamental Photographs; 111 (bl), Russ Lappa/Photo Researchers, Inc.; 111 (bc), Lester V. Bergman/Corbis–Bettmann; 111 (tl), Sally Anderson–Bruce/HRW; 112 (bc, br), Richard Megna/Fundamental Photographs; 12 (bl), Tom Pantages Photography; 113 (br), HRW; 113 (tr), Sam Dudgeon/HRW; 114 (bl), Charles D. Winters/Photo Researchers, Inc.; 114 (bc, br), Richard Megna/Fundamental Photographs; 115 (tr), Sam Dudgeon/HRW; 116 (tl, cl), Sam Dudgeon/HRW; 116 (tr), ©1990 P. Petersen/Custom Medical Stock Photo; 116 (tc, bl), Victoria Smith/HRW; 117 (cr), Phillip Hayson/Photo Researchers, Inc.; 117 (br), Sam Dudgeon/HRW; 118 (tl), Sam Dudgeon/HRW; 118 (b), CORBIS Images/HRW; 119 (tl, tc), Richard Megna/Fundamental Photographs; 119 (tr), Charlie Winters/HRW; 120 (bl), NASA; 120 (tl), © Jeff Greenberg/Visuals Unlimited ; 121 (tr), Sam Dudgeon/HRW; 122 (b), Sam Dudgeon/HRW; 123 (br), John Langford/HRW; 124 (tl), Sam Dudgeon/HRW; 128 (tr), CORBIS Images/HRW; 129 (cr), © Lawrence Berkeley National Laboratory/Photo Researchers, Inc.; 129 (cl), © Bettmann/CORBIS

Lab Book/Appendix "LabBook Header", "L", Corbis Images; "a", Letraset Phototone; "b", and "B", HRW; "o", and "k", images ©2006 PhotoDisc/HRW; 130 (all), Sam Dudgeon/HRW; 131 (tr), John Langford/HRW; 131 (cr), NASA; 132 (all), Sam Dudgeon/HRW; 133 (br), Sam Dudgeon/HRW; 134 (bl), Sam Dudgeon/HRW; 135 (br), Sam Dudgeon/HRW; 137 (bc), Sam Dudgeon/HRW; 138 (br), Gareth Trevor/Getty Images; 139 (tr), Sam Dudgeon/HRW; 144 (br), Victoria Smith; 145 (br), Victoria Smith; 151 (tr), Peter Van Steen/HRW; 151 (br), Sam Dudgeon/HRW; 165 (tr), Sam Dudgeon/HRW